ON THIS ROCK

A Study of Peter's Life and Ministry

Joseph S. Wang and Anne B. Crumpler

Abingdon Press
Nashville

ON THIS ROCK: A STUDY OF PETER'S LIFE AND MINISTRY
Revised Edition

ISBN 0-687-08558-6

This book is printed on acid-free paper.

MANUFACTURED IN THE UNITED STATES OF AMERICA.

98 99 00 01 02 03 04 05 06 07–10 9 8 7 6 5 4 3 2 1

Contents

A Word About the Writers

Dr. Joseph S. Wang is from Taiwan and has been an American citizen since 1972. He holds a degree in electrical engineering from National Taiwan University, a B.D. degree in biblical literature from Asbury Theological Seminary, a Th.M. degree from Princeton Theological Seminary, and a Ph.D. degree from Emory University. Dr. Wang is a professor of New Testament at Asbury Theological Seminary.

Anne B. Crumpler comes from a long line of ministers and grew up on dinner-table theology. She has a bachelor's degree in philosophy and religion and a master's degree in religious education. Ms. Crumpler has been an assistant editor at The United Methodist Publishing House and is now a freelance writer and editor. She is a ruling elder in the Presbyterian Church and teaches an adult Sunday school class.

A Word of Welcome

Welcome to ON THIS ROCK: A STUDY OF PETER'S LIFE AND MINISTRY.

Personal stories are one of the most easily accessible tools for relating information and insights from the human experience. The Bible is full of stories about how the community of faith faced life and death issues as well as the everyday comings and goings of daily existence.

Some stories are deceptively simple. Someone said or did this, someone else responded by doing or saying that. End of story, we think. But is that all that happened? What happened next? What feelings did each person experience? Did anyone know that? Who else heard or saw the transaction? Were they affected in any way? Did the principal players know their interaction had any impact on someone else?

Peter Would Be Astounded!

No doubt the apostle Peter would be amazed, perhaps dismayed, that two thousand years later anyone even knew what he had said or done, much less used it as a means to understand the Christian faith! Yet that is exactly what we will do with this study about Peter's life and ministry.

Many of us are familiar with some of these stories of Peter: How Jesus called him to be a disciple; how he experienced the exhilaration of seeing two giants of the faith appear miraculously with Jesus at the Transfiguration; how he sank in despair and desperation after having denied Jesus three times following his vehement insistence of loyalty at any cost. We may be less familiar with some of the details of his personal and home life, which are actually much like our own.

During this study of Peter, we will follow him from his call through his confession of Jesus as Lord; his life of discipleship; his experiences in the Transfiguration, the arrest of Jesus, the Resurrection and post-Resurrection; his bold expression at Pentecost; and his life as a missionary to the Gentiles and others in the days of the early church. We will discover that his life, while lived centuries ago, was in many respects very much like our own and that we have much to learn from him.

A Successful Study

ON THIS ROCK is a self-contained study with all the teaching/learning suggestions conveniently located in the margin next to or near the main text to which they refer. In addition to your Bible, all you need to have a successful group or individual study session is provided for you in this book.

Most of the discussion and reflection questions are addressed to "you," since learners and leaders will have the same book. Some of the questions invite group members to discover what the Bible or the session text says and means. Others ask for some analysis or imaginative thinking. Some ask for learners to tap their own experience, to think about what it meant and how it felt to them, and what the results were. In many instances you will be invited to think about your commitment to Jesus Christ as you consider what lessons Peter has taught you about a life of discipleship.

We invite you further to delve deeply into this old-but-new story of Peter and to open yourself to his example of dedication and discipleship. Like Peter, we have flaws and foibles, but we are also daily invited by Jesus to "feed my sheep." Many blessings to you in your own journey of discipleship.

Session One

First of the Apostles

Read Matthew 10:1-4; Mark 3:13-19; Luke 6:12-16.

Session Focus ■

We have questions about what discipleship means. Understanding Peter and his relationship to Jesus may help us to grow as disciples of Christ.

Session Objective ■

To begin to relate to Peter who was, like us, an ordinary person in need of salvation.

Session Preparation ■

Read the Scripture. Read through the material in this chapter. Obtain one or more books of names.

Session Outline ■

Choose from among these activities and discussion starters.

One of the most fascinating characters in the New Testament is Simon Peter, one of the twelve apostles of Jesus. Most of us can easily identify with Peter. He represents humankind in its length, breadth, depth, and height more than any other person in the New Testament.

We can see reflections of the image of our own lives in Peter's life. He was an ordinary man. He was not very profound, yet he was not stupid. He was impulsive and uninhibited. He liked to talk and act without careful thought, although sometimes he would think through issues in detail. He made mistakes frequently. In his good intentions, he would make promises that he often failed to keep. Peter thought big and wanted to do great things for the Lord and his kingdom. But often Peter was unsuccessful in carrying these ideas to completion. He was a man of faith and a man of doubt. Sometimes he was brave; sometimes he was a coward. Peter was very much human as we are.

The life of Peter is fascinating not only because he was very human like the rest of us but also because in his life we can see the working of God's grace. God took such an ordinary man and made him one of the greatest and most effective leaders in the

New Testament church. If we will trust ourselves in God's hand, God can also take us, ordinary persons, and make us effective and useful in God's kingdom.

"Simon, Whom He Named Peter"

The New Testament uses four different names for Peter. These are *Simeon*, *Simon*, *Peter*, and *Cephas*.

Simeon was Peter's Hebrew name. He was known by this name in Jewish Christian circles. James, brother of the Lord and leader of the Jerusalem church, referred to Peter by this name (Acts 15:14). Originally the Jews spoke the Hebrew language. Most of the Old Testament is written in Hebrew. After the Jews were taken into captivity in Babylon (about six centuries before Christ) and in New Testament times, they spoke Aramaic. But many people in the first century still used Hebrew names.

Simon is the Greek form of *Simeon*. During New Testament times, Greek was widely used in commerce, politics, and the arts. So, many people in Palestine either had two names, one Hebrew (or Aramaic) and one Greek, or two forms of the same name, one Hebrew and one Greek.

Jesus gave Simon a new name, *Cephas*, which in Aramaic means "rock." *Peter* is the Greek form of *Cephas*.

Work, Home, and Family

Peter's hometown was Bethsaida (John 1:44). Bethsaida means "house of hunting or fishing." The town is located near the mouth of the Jordan River, about two miles east of the river. The best fishing grounds are found near the mouth of the River Jordan, at the northeast edge of the Sea of Galilee.

Peter's father was called "Jonah" by

"Simon, Whom He Named Peter" ■

Look up your name in a book of names. What does it mean?

Think about the kind of person you are and your place in the church. What name would you choose for yourself? What name would Jesus choose for you?

Work, Home, and Family ■

Where do you live? Who are the people in your family? What is your occupation?

Discuss: In what ways are you defined by your home? work? family?

Matthew (16:17) and "John" by John the Evangelist (1:42; 21:15-17). Peter had a brother by the name of Andrew. Both Peter and Andrew were fishermen by trade, and both later became disciples of Jesus. Two sons of Zebedee, James and John, probably were their partners in the fishing business (Luke 5:10). Fishing was a very important industry around the Sea of Galilee at that time.

During the Galilean ministry of Jesus, Peter owned a house in Capernaum. Peter was married, and his mother-in-law lived with him and his wife. Peter's brother Andrew also lived with them in the same house (Mark 1:29-30). Jesus seemed to have used this house as his headquarters in Capernaum.

First Among the Twelve

First Among the Twelve ■
Read Matthew 10:2-4.

Peter had a prominent position in the circle of twelve apostles. He is listed first in lists of the Twelve in the New Testament (Matthew 10:2-4; Mark 3:16-19; Luke 6:13-16; Acts 1:13). In the Gospels, he is the most frequently mentioned of the Twelve. He was one of the inner circle of disciples who accompanied Jesus on some special occasions. When Jesus raised the daughter of Jairus, he took Peter, James, and John into the room with him (Mark 5:37; Luke 8:51). These three witnessed the Transfiguration of Jesus (Matthew 17:1-8). During his agonizing experience in Gethsemane, Jesus took only these three with him into the garden (Matthew 26:37; Mark 14:33).

Discuss: What kind of person would be first among the disciples?

Look up some of the Bible passages mentioned in this section. What do these references teach you about discipleship?

Do you have a way of segregating duty from privilege as Peter seemed to? Does Peter's way seem appropriate? Explain.

Often Peter served as the spokesman for the twelve apostles. He was perceptive. He was concerned, interested not only in himself but in others as well. These qualities made him a leader among the apostles. At Caesarea Philippi, Jesus asked the disciples who they thought he was. Peter spoke for them and said, "You are the Messiah, the Son of the living God" (Matthew 16:16). Peter often spoke to Jesus for the other disciples: "Explain this parable to us" (Matthew 15:15); "Lord, are you telling this parable for us or for everyone?" (Luke 12:41). After Jesus cursed the fig tree, it was Peter who called Jesus' attention, "Rabbi, look! The fig tree that you cursed has withered" (Mark 11:21).

Peter had a way of thinking about something Jesus said, dropping out of the conversation, so to speak, and then coming in a little while later with a relevant question on the subject, from which Jesus had passed. In Matthew 18:15-17, Jesus taught the disciples how to deal with a member who went wrong. Then Jesus went on to speak about prayer and Christian fellowship (Matthew 18:19-20). Peter was not paying attention to the latter. He was still thinking about Jesus' earlier comments. So he broke in and asked Jesus about the first issue: "Lord, if another member of the church sins against me, how often should I forgive? As many as seven times?" (Matthew 18:21).

Impulsive Faith

Another major character trait of Peter is that he was impulsive. He often spoke and acted impetuously. Once Peter discovered that Jesus was walking on the sea as the apostles fought against the storm in their boat. So Peter asked Jesus to bid him to walk on the water too. Jesus did so, and Peter got out of the boat and into the water (Matthew 14:28-29). After Peter's great conversion at Caesarea Philippi, Jesus began to teach the disciples about his coming suffering. Immediately Peter rebuked Jesus for having such thoughts (Matthew 16:22). On the mountain of Transfiguration, Peter proposed

Impulsive Faith ■

Peter was enthusiastic about his faith, so he sometimes acted or spoke first and thought about it later.

Reflect: When have you found faith exciting? overwhelming? When have you failed to be faithful?

to build there three dwellings—one each for Moses, Elijah, and Jesus (Matthew 17:4). At Capernaum when the collectors of the half-shekel temple poll tax asked Peter, "Does your teacher not pay the temple tax?" Peter impetuously answered, "Yes, he does." Later Jesus had to tell Peter that, being the Son of God, he did not have to pay that tax (Matthew 17:25-27). At the Last Supper, Peter would not allow Jesus to wash his feet at first. When Jesus explained the significance of washing his feet, immediately Peter requested that Jesus wash his whole body (John 13:6-9). When Jesus predicted that after his arrest the disciples would fall away, Peter impetuously responded, "Even though all become deserters, I will not" (Mark 14:29). At the scene of Jesus' arrest, Peter used a sword to defend Jesus and cut off the ear of the high priest's servant (John 18:10). Yet only a few hours later Peter denied Jesus three times (Matthew 26:69-75).

These incidents well illustrate Peter's personality. He would say something impetuously, make some promise, or start to do something. Yet he often failed to carry through. When he attempted to walk on the water, he began with a bold demonstration of faith. But soon the swelling waves frightened him and he lost his faith (Matthew 14:28-31).

How many of us are like that! How many of us can identify with Peter in these personality traits! How often we would impulsively do something or commit ourselves to some project yet be unable to complete it.

Peter failed many times. But whenever he failed, he always repented and returned to the Lord. He always sincerely desired to be loyal to the Lord, even though he might have performed badly.

Look up several of the Bible references to Peter's impetuousness. What do these references teach you about commitment? about faithful follow-through?

Do you think it is better to start and falter than never to start at all? Explain.

Leadership by the Grace of God ■

Who are the leaders in your church? What makes them leaders?

Picture in your mind the person in your church least likely to be a leader. Remember that God chooses the most unlikely people to proclaim the Word.

Leadership by the Grace of God

The grace of God took such an ordinary, weak vessel and made him very useful and effective in God's kingdom. The first half of the Book of Acts describes Peter's vital leadership in the emerging church. He boldly addressed the crowd on the Day of Pentecost and was instrumental in bringing three thousand souls into the church. Later, five thousand more souls were brought to Christ through Peter's ministry. The early church grew and expanded through his ministry. God accomplished great things through Peter.

Why Bother With Peter? ■

Make a list of questions you have about discipleship. At the end of each session, consider how learning about Peter has helped answer your questions.

Are you ever confused about what you believe? (This is OK!) What helps bring clarity?

Why Bother With Peter?

Christians ask questions: What does it mean to follow Jesus? What is discipleship? What should we believe? How should we act?

We attempt answers: Following Jesus is being like Christ. Being a disciple means living a Christian life, following the Golden Rule, loving neighbors, encouraging others to be open to the will of God, maybe bringing a friend to church. We believe in God and Jesus and the Holy Spirit. We should act in ways that reflect what we believe; holiness is a personal witness to the presence of Christ in our lives.

The truth is that we are sometimes thoroughly confused about what we believe and about how disciples of Christ should act.

According to the tradition of the church, Simon Peter was the quintessential disciple. Perhaps if we find out more about Peter, we can begin to answer some of our questions.

Nothing Special ■

What do you think: Were Jesus' disciples extraordinary? Why? Why not?

Nothing Special

Actually, Peter was a pretty ordinary person. He had a home, a family, a job. Peter was a lot like us. If he lived in the United

What do you think is the "average" disciple today? Do you think Jesus would be pleased? Explain.

States today, he would probably exemplify the census bureau's portrait of an average man: thirty-four years old, high school diploma and maybe some college, living with his family in an urban area in a home he owns, working as a manager or an administrator for about $45,000 a year, affiliated with a Christian church. If Peter were around today, he'd be a lot like us.

Peter was impulsive. He blurted out half-formed thoughts. He leapt into life with uninhibited enthusiasm. He made a fool of himself every time he turned around. Peter was not insightful. He did not understand Jesus.

Asked to defend his faith, Peter failed. "Me—a disciple of Jesus? I never knew the guy."

Maybe we should look elsewhere for a model of Christian discipleship.

A Model of Discipleship

A Model of Discipleship ■

Tell Bible stories about Peter. What do you remember?

Look up the Bible passages in this section. What is it about Peter that stands out? Why do you suppose Jesus called Peter to be a disciple? Why do the Gospels list him first among the Twelve?

Still, Peter was first among the apostles. Though each Gospel puts a slightly different spin on Peter's character and his place in the ministry of Jesus Christ, all agree that he was prominent among the companions of Jesus and a leader in the early church. "These are the names of the twelve apostles:" says Matthew (10:2), "first, Simon, also known as Peter." What about Peter made him first among the apostles? What made him a model of discipleship?

Some would argue that Peter had the necessary qualities of faith and leadership. He was, after all, spokesman both for the disciples and for the church in Jerusalem. But if we look at the Gospel accounts of Peter's discipleship, little commends him, except perhaps his enthusiastic faith. And even his enthusiasm tends to backfire. In Matthew

14:22-32, he attempts to walk on the water to Jesus, but he loses faith (and nerve) and sinks. At the Last Supper, he passionately stands his ground (Mark 14:31); but not long afterward, he denies he ever knew Jesus. Peter was, in Jesus' estimation, a man "of little faith" (Matthew 14:31). Why do we look to him as first among the faithful?

Others say that Jesus saw in Peter qualities that made him a leader among the apostles—qualities that no one else saw. Jesus called him, saying, "Follow me and I will make you fish for people" (Mark 1:17). In the Gospel of Matthew, Jesus names him *Peter*, which means "rock," and tells him, "You are Peter, and on this rock I will build my church" (Matthew 16:18). Apparently, Jesus had confidence that Peter would become a missionary and a leader in the church. But did Peter have extraordinary leadership abilities? Maybe. Maybe not.

What is it that stands out about Peter? What is it that makes him first among the apostles?

First But Not Alone

First But Not Alone ■

Peter was part of the community of faith. He was not a hero; he did not stand alone.

What does the community of faith mean in your life? What does it mean for your faith?

Peter is first among the disciples. All the Gospels write his name at the top of the list. But Peter never stands alone. In almost every situation, he is part of the community. He stands with the disciples and speaks for them. In the Synoptic Gospels (Matthew, Mark, Luke), he is part of the group of disciples closest to Jesus, the inner circle. In John, he is pictured with the beloved disciple. At Pentecost, "they were all together in one place" (Acts 2:1) and "Peter, standing with the eleven, raised his voice and addressed" the people (2:14). Peter was part of the community of the faithful.

God's Saving Love ■

Read Luke 22:31-32 and John 21:15-19. How does Jesus minister to Peter? Does this strengthen you? How?

As you continue in this course, attempt to describe Peter's relationship to Jesus. How does it change?

Write a brief description of your relationship to Jesus.

At the end of this course, consider how your relationship has changed.

God's Saving Love

If we look at the stories of Peter, we see an ordinary man, badly in need of salvation.

The Gospel of Mark emphasizes the fact that Peter misunderstands Jesus and finally denies him. Matthew focuses on Peter's need to be saved. (Peter walks on water and sinks; Jesus saves him.) Luke, who tries his best to cover Peter's faults, includes Jesus' prayer for Peter: "Satan has demanded to sift all of you like wheat, but I have prayed for you that your own faith may not fail; and you, when once you have turned back, strengthen your brothers" (Luke 22:31-32). Peter denies him. Only because of Jesus' faith does he repent and return. In John, Jesus calls Peter to "feed my sheep," but puts his call to ministry in the context of love: "Do you love me?" (John 21:17).

Peter is first among the disciples because he resides in the saving love of God through Jesus Christ. Even in the Book of Acts, which describes Peter's ministry in the church, Peter relies on God's salvation.

Peter is not the model of Christian discipleship because of his leadership qualities or even because of his faith. Peter is a model of discipleship because he is nothing special. He is a lot like us. But Jesus saves him, chooses him, calls him, commissions him, and loves him.

So What?

As we look for answers to our questions, we can in fact look to Peter as a model of discipleship. He was a lot like us. He was not especially holy. He did not follow the rules. When it came to faith and practice, Peter did everything wrong.

But Peter was loved and called and commissioned by Jesus Christ. And so are we. As we look further into Peter's life, we may discover that our lives of Christian discipleship begin to take shape.

Prayer ■

Thank you, God, for disciples like Peter who help us learn to follow Jesus. Amen.

First of the Apostles **15**

Session Two

The Call of Peter

Read Matthew 4:18-22; Mark 1:16-20; Luke 5:1-11; John 1:35-42.

Session Focus ■
This session looks at Peter's call to discipleship as a call to become part of God's new creation.

Session Objective ■
To understand discipleship in relationship to the new people of God.

Session Preparation ■
Read the Scripture. Read through the material in this chapter. Have available copies of the order of worship used in your church.

Session Outline ■
Choose from among these activities and discussion questions.

In the Gospel of John, Jesus passed by the place where John the Baptist was baptizing. John saw Jesus and said, "Here is the Lamb of God who takes away the sin of the world! . . . This is the Son of God" (John 1:29, 34). Two disciples of John heard this statement and followed Jesus. They stayed with Jesus that day and came to realize that he was the Messiah. One of these two was Andrew, who went and found his brother Peter, told him that he had found the Messiah, and brought him to meet Jesus.

Peter's hometown was Bethsaida (John 1:44) of Galilee. When Andrew found him, Peter was not in his home territory but in Judea. In those days traveling was not easy and convenient. One would not travel unless the journey was necessary and important. Probably Peter, like other Jews of his time, was eagerly looking for the coming of the Messiah. When he heard about the ministry of John the Baptist he became interested. So he went to the place where John was preaching and baptizing. Possibly he too was a follower of John the Baptist. Since he was eagerly awaiting the coming of the Messiah, Peter was ready to go to meet him when Andrew said, "We have found the Messiah."

A New Name ■

Peter's new name was an indication that he was a new person with a new relationship to God and with a new role among God's people.

When are times that people commonly change their names? Have you changed your name? If so, why? Did it signal a new role for you?

Do you know of other people who have changed their names? Why did they make the change?

A New Name

When Peter came to Jesus, Jesus looked at him carefully. In the New Testament the Greek word translated "look" here means to gaze in a concentrated, intent manner. Such a gaze does not mean seeing only the superficial things that lie on the surface but reading a person's heart. Jesus gazed into the inner being of Peter and said to him: " 'You are Simon son of John. You are to be called Cephas' (which is translated Peter)" (John 1:42). *Peter* is the Greek and *Cephas* is the Aramaic word for a rock. So *Peter* and *Cephas* are not different names; they are the same name in two different languages.

So Jesus gave Simon a new name. In the Old Testament when a person enters into a new relationship with God, or when a person assumes a new role, that one will have a new name. Jesus was saying Peter would become a new man, assume a new role in God's kingdom. The ordinary Simon would become a strong and steady rock in Christ's church (see Matthew 16:18-19).

When Jesus Christ looks at a person, he sees not only who she or he is, he also sees what that person can become. He sees not only the actualities in a person, but also the possibilities. Jesus Christ can release the potential in a person and help that one become what he or she can become, if that person is willing to commit herself or himself to Christ.

Fishing for People ■

Read Mark 1:16-20 or Matthew 4:18-20. What was Peter doing before Jesus called him? What did Jesus call him to do? What does it mean to fish for people?

Fishing for People

In Matthew, Mark, and Luke, Jesus began his ministry in Galilee. Early in his Galilean ministry Jesus met Peter and Andrew fishing in the Sea of Galilee. Jesus said to them, "Follow me, and I will make you fish for people" (Matthew 4:19). This was a call to

If you had been Peter, would you have followed Jesus? What would you want to know first? What do you or would you do to fish for people?

permanent discipleship. It was not a call to discipleship like that any other master in Israel offered. It was not merely to learn more of doctrine, nor was it to complete a life direction already taken. This call was a challenge to become something quite new—fishers of people. This new call could not have been addressed to Peter and Andrew unless they had already known Jesus and understood something of his mission. Peter and Andrew heard this call and became his permanent disciples (Matthew 4:18-20; Mark 1:16-20).

Full Nets ■

Read Luke 5:1-11. Identify the miracle, the confession, and the call.

Reflect: How did Peter respond to Jesus? How do you respond to the presence of Christ in your life?

Full Nets

In Luke 5:1-11, Luke gives us a more detailed report of Jesus' calling Peter to full-time discipleship. According to Luke, a great number of people gathered together by the shore of the Lake of Gennesaret, another name for the Sea of Galilee. Since many people were there, Jesus got into Peter's boat and asked him to put out a little from the land. Jesus sat down and taught the people from the boat.

After the lesson, Jesus told Peter to sail to the deep part of the sea and let down the nets for a catch of fish. Peter was an experienced fisherman. He knew that nighttime was the best time for fishing, not morning. In response to Jesus' direction Peter said, "Master, we have worked all night long but have caught nothing. Yet if you say so, I will let down the nets" (Luke 5:5). At this point Peter knew a little bit of Jesus' power. So he, an experienced fisherman, was willing to follow the direction of a carpenter regarding fishing. When they let down the net, it enclosed a great quantity of fish. As a result the nets were in danger of bursting. They beckoned to their partners in the other boat

Is your response like Peter's? Why? Why not? When, if ever, have you been seized by wonder combined with fear? If you have ever felt overwhelmed by the presence of God, have you wanted God "to go away"?

to come and help them. They filled both the boats with fish, and the boats began to sink.

When Peter saw this, he fell down at Jesus' knees and said, "Go away from me, Lord, for I am a sinful man" (Luke 5:8). Peter had witnessed as Jesus performed miracles several times before. Yet when Jesus performed a miracle in Peter's own field of labor, Peter was overwhelmed. Luke 5:9 says that Peter was amazed. However, in the original Greek language Luke says *thambos* seized Peter. The Greek word means "wonder combined with fear," perhaps containing recognition of the presence of the divine.

Have you experienced a new stage of life as Peter did? Describe that experience and the results.

Peter recognized that he was in the presence of God. Earlier he addressed Jesus as "Master" (Luke 5:5) but now as "Lord" (Luke 5:8). This word "Lord" (Greek word *Kyrios*) is constantly used of God in the Greek translation of the Old Testament and is commonly used in many religions to refer to deity. Peter obeyed the command of the master earlier, but now he fell down at the knees of the Lord, whose holiness causes agony to the sinner. The first natural reaction of a person under such circumstances is to feel that she or he cannot exist before the Holy One. Consequently Peter cried out impulsively, "Go away from me, Lord, for I am a sinful man!" Peter was not requesting Jesus to leave him permanently; he was expressing his own unworthiness.

Look at your church's order of worship. In what ways does the order of worship follow a pattern similar to the call of Peter? (For example, many churches begin worship with an invocation, a prayer asking Christ to be present.)

To this Jesus responded by saying to Peter, "Do not be afraid; from now on you will be catching people" (Luke 5:10). The phrase *from now on* indicates that Peter was about to begin a new stage of life. When a person meets Jesus in a fresh way, that person begins a new stage of life. The Greek word for "catch" is *zogreo*, which literally means "to take alive" or to save persons alive from danger. Jesus would make Peter save persons alive from spiritual danger. At this Peter left everything and became a full-time disciple of Jesus.

One of the Twelve ■

Do you have any sense of yourself as an ambassador for Jesus Christ? Read Mark 3:14-15.

In your role in the church, do you feel that if someone rejects or accepts your gifts and/or leadership that it is the same thing as rejecting or accepting Jesus Christ? Explain.

One of the Twelve

Later in his ministry, Jesus selected from among many of his followers twelve to be with him. He appointed them and sent them out to preach and have authority over demons (Mark 3:14-15). Those twelve were called apostles. They were men through whom Jesus Christ himself would accomplish his work on earth, after his ascension to heaven. They were to be his official ambassadors commissioned by him to carry out specific assignments. They were to be such representatives of Jesus that he who accepts or rejects them accepts or rejects Christ himself. They were to be the leaders of the early church. Peter was called, selected, and appointed to this crucial rank.

"Follow Me" ■

Read Genesis 12:1-4. In what ways is the call to Peter like the call to Abram? Make a list.

"Follow Me"

Matthew and Mark tell the same story about Peter's call. Jesus saw Simon, "who is called Peter," and his brother, Andrew, fishing by the Sea of Galilee. He called to them, "Follow me, and I will make you fish for people" (Matthew 4:19). Immediately, they stopped what they were doing and followed Jesus.

The story of Peter's call sounds a lot like the call of Abram. (Read Genesis 12:1-4.) God called Abram: "Go to the land that I will show you. . . . So Abram went." Jesus said, "Follow me," and Peter followed. It's likely that the Gospel writers expected their readers to remember God's call to Abram. God made a covenant with Abram and his descendants. They would be God's people.

God established a *new* covenant through Jesus Christ. Peter would be the first of the new people of God.

Jesus spoke with divine authority: "Follow me." Peter and Andrew didn't ask questions. They simply "left their nets and followed him" (Mark 1:18). Had Peter heard of Jesus? We don't know. We do know that when Jesus called, Peter followed.

Jesus' call was also a commissioning. Jesus gave Peter a job to do: "I will make you fish for people" (Mark 1:17). Peter would become a missionary in the early church.

So far, we know nothing about Peter's character; but we know a little more about Christian discipleship. Peter's call marked the beginning of Jesus' ministry, the beginning of a new covenant and a new people. Peter was called to play a particular role in the church: fishing for people. We know that Jesus spoke with authority, calling Peter to discipleship and defining his future.

Peter was called to be part of a new creation and bound by a new covenant. So are we. Read Jeremiah 31:33-34 and 2 Corinthians 5:16-21.

Discuss: What does it mean to be part of a new creation? What is the new covenant? What is your part in that covenant?

Miracles

Luke tells a different story. The beginning of the Gospel tells of Jesus' birth, when Mary joined a host of angels singing praises to God for the coming of the Messiah. This Messiah has "brought down the powerful from their thrones, / and lifted up the lowly; / he has filled the hungry with good things, / and sent the rich away empty" (Luke 1:52-53). Jesus began his ministry teaching, proclaiming God's kingdom: good news to the poor, release to the captives, sight to the blind, freedom for the oppressed (see Luke 4:18). Then the miracles began. Miracles are signs of the Kingdom; they are the same as proclaiming health for the sick or full bellies for the hungry. The story of Peter's call is set in the context of God's kingdom.

Miracles ▪

Read Luke 4:18. Use words or pictures to describe the kingdom of God.

Peter was called to proclaim the good news of God's kingdom. So are we. Write a paragraph or a short speech proclaiming the good news of God's kingdom.

The Call of Peter **21**

Read Luke 5:1-11. Do you think this large catch was a miracle? Explain. Is "catching people" a miracle? Why or why not?

Peter had come in from fishing all night. Jesus told him to go out into the deep water and to let down his nets again. Who would do such a crazy thing? Everyone—including Peter—knew that fishing in the daytime was a waste of time and energy. We can't help but sense the sarcasm or at least the weariness in his voice: "Master, . . . If you say so, I will let down the nets" (Luke 5:5). But the nets filled to the breaking point and almost sank the boats.

The kingdom of God happens unexpectedly. It is like catching fish in broad daylight. Peter sees nets full to overflowing and knows that he is in the presence of the Messiah, who brings in God's kingdom.

Do you believe that miracles happen today? Have you benefited from a miracle? Explain.

Peter responds to the miracle of the full nets by confessing his sins, "Go away from me, Lord, for I am a sinful man!" (Luke 5:8). In the presence of divinity, the only possible response is confession.

Then Jesus said to Simon, " 'Do not be afraid; from now on you will be catching people.' When they had brought their boats to shore, they left everything and followed him" (Luke 5:10-11)

We still know little of Peter's character. We do know that he was called to proclaim the good news of God's kingdom. Peter's call is evangelical; he is to "catch people," to haul them in like fish, in nets that would be empty—if it weren't for Jesus, the Messiah.

Cephas: Peter ■

Read John 1:35-42. Peter came to Jesus as a response to the witness of his brother Andrew. When did you first hear about Jesus? How did you respond?

Cephas: Peter

The Gospel of John begins with John the Baptist witnessing to the Messiah. He saw Jesus and announced, "Here is the Lamb of God who takes away the sin of the world!" (John 1:29). Two of John's disciples heard John's testimony and followed Jesus.

Jesus turned to them and asked, "What are

Describe a situation in which you told another person about Jesus. What did you say?

When Jesus says to you, "Come and see," what do you see? How are you drawn to respond to what you see? Are you satisfied with that response? Would Jesus be satisfied?

When he met Jesus, Peter was changed. Even his name was changed. In what ways are we changed by Jesus?

you looking for?" But they had no answer. They were not willing to make a commitment, not yet. (Or perhaps John wants the reader to know that disciples are pretty unclear about who they are and what they hope for.) "Rabbi, where are you staying?" they ask. Jesus answers, "Come and see," and they spend the day with him. One of the men is Andrew, who tells his brother, Simon, "We have found the Messiah." Simon went with Andrew to Jesus.

The dialogue tells the story: "Here is the Lamb of God." "What are you looking for?" "Come and see." "We have found the Messiah." The two disciples followed Jesus because they heard the testimony of John the Baptist. Peter went to Jesus because of Andrew's testimony. In the Gospel of John, Jesus gathers in God's people through word of mouth. The stories of faith include witness—Jesus is the Messiah—and invitation—"Come and see."

Jesus looked at Simon and said to him, " 'You are Simon son of John. You are to be called Cephas' (which is translated Peter)" (John 1:42). The Gospel writer wants us to remember the importance of names. Abram was named Abraham, the father of a multitude; Jacob became Israel, the man who has seen God. Simon, which means "heard," becomes Peter, which means "rock." Meeting God changes people. Simon, who heard the testimony, became a new person in relationship to Jesus. He needed a new name. Jesus named and defined him: Peter.

Again, we know little about Peter, but we know more about Christian discipleship. Peter was called to faith by word of mouth. Peter heard the word, and in relationship to Jesus, was changed.

So What? ■
Describe Peter's relationship to Jesus. How has learning about Peter helped to answer your questions about discipleship? How has learning about Peter helped you to commit yourself to discipleship?

So What?

We sing, "I can hear my Savior calling.... Where he leads me I will follow." Jesus does, in fact, call us to be disciples. The stories of Peter's call begin to show us what it means to follow Jesus.

Like Peter, we are called to be a part of Jesus' ministry, which means that we are part of God's new people and God's new covenant. Like Peter, we are given jobs to do. Peter was called to fish for people, to be a missionary and an evangelist. We are called to proclaim God's kingdom: good news to the poor, release to the captives, sight to the blind, freedom to the oppressed. Like Peter, we hear the good news and we spread the word: "We have found the Messiah."

Christian discipleship isn't easy. Left to our own devices, we wouldn't follow Jesus. But apparently discipleship isn't up to us. Jesus said, "Follow me," and Peter followed. Hearing the word, Peter went to Jesus and was changed. He became a new person: Peter, a disciple of Christ. Like Peter, we hear the word. We're tentative about Jesus; but when we meet him, we are changed and renamed: Christian.

Prayer ■
God, make us disciples, like Peter, who are part of your new creation and bound by the new covenant in Jesus Christ. Amen.

Peter's Confession

Read Matthew 16:13-20; Mark 8:27-30; Luke 9:18-20.

Caesarea Philippi was a great center of pagan religions. The area was scattered with temples of the ancient Syrian Baal worship. Here also are the upper sources of the Jordan River. Herod the Great built a great temple of white marble here to the godhead of Caesar. When his son, Philip received governance of the tetrarchy, he enriched the temple, beautified the town, and changed the name of the city from Panias to Caesarea in honor of Caesar, who was considered a god.

The visit by Jesus and his disciples to Caesarea Philippi may have initially been a discouraging one, since Jesus had spent most of his time in Gentile regions, strongholds of what faithful Jews would consider pagan religions. When Jesus had been in Jewish territory, he had wrangled with the Pharisees and Sadducees, who thought that he was undermining the tradition and laws of the elders. What was on his mind? What was he trying to do?

Who Do People Say That I Am?

Jesus asked the disciples two very important questions. First he asked them, "Who do people say that I am?" (Mark 8:27).

They told him, "John the Baptist; and others, Elijah; and still others, one of the

Who Do People Say That I Am? ■

If Jesus had asked this question of you when you were new to the faith, what would you have said?

prophets" (Mark 8:28). These men all agreed in considering Jesus' mission as straight from heaven. Yet they did not consider him to be the Messiah.

Jesus asked the first question not to solicit the information but to prepare the apostles for the second question and to help the Twelve crystallize their own thoughts. At this point, Jesus knew that the end of his earthly ministry was drawing near. He needed to instruct the apostles in the real nature of his ministry and that of the Kingdom so that they would be prepared to carry on the ministry. Before he could take this important step, the apostles would need to know who he really was. This was indispensable, particularly in view of their perplexity. To help the apostles come to grips with this truth, Jesus asked them the second question, "But who do you say that I am?" (Mark 8:29).

Jesus Christ, Son of God ■

Read aloud one or more of the creeds of the church. What do the creeds say about Jesus?

Jesus Christ, Son of God

Peter answered, "You are the Messiah, the Son of the living God" (Matthew 16:16). *Messiah* is from the Hebrew word meaning "anointed." Its equivalent in Greek is *christ.* In the Old Testament, kings, priests (particularly high priests), and sometimes prophets were anointed. These were anointed ones. They were christs, messiahs. Peter did not say, "You are a messiah." But emphatically he declared, "You are *the* Messiah."

Peter identified Jesus as the unique one God had promised to send, whose coming the Old Testament prophets awaited. The Jews awaited the Messiah, but they did not understand the Messiah to be divine. They only thought the Messiah would possess some supernatural powers. Yet Peter confessed Jesus to be the Son of the living God. Some people were called "son of God" by

Using a Bible dictionary, look up "son of God." How is Jesus unique as the Son of God?

virtue of their office. For example, kings and judges were called "son of God."

Peter did not mean Jesus was a son of God by virtue of his official position. Peter declared Jesus to be the unique Son of the living God. Jesus was actually divine. Only the confession of this high view of the person of Jesus could have induced such response from Jesus. Jesus had earlier referred to God as "my Father in heaven" (Matthew 10:32). The disciples had already recognized Jesus as the Messiah. Here Peter confessed Jesus' divine sonship.

Jesus answered Peter, "Blessed are you, Simon son of Jonah! For flesh and blood has not revealed this to you, but my Father in heaven. And I tell you, you are Peter, and on this rock I will build my church, and the gates of Hades will not prevail against it. I will give you the keys of the kingdom of heaven, and whatever you bind on earth will be bound in heaven, and whatever you loose on earth will be loosed in heaven" (Matthew 16:17-19).

On This Rock ■

Jesus builds the community of faith on Peter and on Peter's faith in Jesus as the Messiah. How do you understand the relationship between *petros* and *petra*?

On This Rock

Interpreters have explained this statement of Jesus many different ways. Jesus said to Peter, "You are Peter [Greek *petros*, meaning a piece of rock], and on this rock [Greek *petra*, meaning a rock-mass] I will build my church." Some claim that the second rock on which Jesus would build his church is exclusively the person of Peter. Others maintain that the second rock refers exclusively to the faith expressed by Peter here. The context, however, seems to indicate that the rock of foundation was both Peter and Peter's faith. The two are inseparable. *Petra* is the bedrock out of which comes *petros*, the individual rock. Peter is the rock that will be molded into a stone of foundation, but he is such because he belongs to and rests upon the bedrock of faith in the Christ.

Notice that it is Jesus, not Peter, who would build the church. The church belongs to Jesus, not to Peter. Peter as the foundation of the church is not to be understood in an absolute sense. First Peter 2:4-8 says Christ is the cornerstone of the church. First Corinthians 3:11 states that Jesus Christ is the foundation of the church. So Peter was to be the foundation of the church in a secondary sense.

Read these five Scripture references, starting with 1 Peter 2:4-8. How would you describe the foundation of the church?

In this sense not only Peter but all the apostles are the foundation of the church. Ephesians 2:19-20 states that the church is "built upon the foundation of the apostles and prophets." Revelation 21:14 mentions that the wall of the new Jerusalem "has twelve foundations, and on them are the twelve names of the twelve apostles of the Lamb." In the prayer in John 17:20 Jesus mentions the new generation of Christians who will believe in him through the word of the apostles. The apostolic foundation of the church is the witness to the death and Resurrection of Jesus Christ and to the identity of the Christ who promises and is exalted. The apostles were the eyewitnesses of the life, death, and Resurrection of Jesus. And Peter was the first and the chief eyewitness.

Discuss: How do you know that Jesus Christ has built your church? In what ways is the church built on you and others in your congregation?

Keys to God's Kingdom

Jesus also told Peter, "I will give you the keys of the kingdom of heaven, and whatever you bind on earth shall be bound in heaven, and whatever you loose on earth shall be loosed in heaven" (Matthew 16:19). Jesus' statement about "keys" elsewhere helps us understand his meaning here. In Luke 11:52 Jesus says, "Woe to you lawyers! For you

Keys to God's Kingdom ■

Jesus gave Peter responsibility for opening or closing the doors to God's kingdom, for allowing access to God. The disciples were given the power to prohibit and to permit, to hold people responsible or to forgive them. Review these four passages about binding, loosing, and keys. Clarify what binding and loosing mean in these contexts—both legislative and judicial. Can you think of examples?

have taken away the key of knowledge; you did not enter yourselves, and you hindered those who were entering." By giving Peter the keys of the kingdom of heaven, Jesus made Peter a steward of the mysteries of the kingdom of God. Later he did the same for the Gentiles.

"Binding" and "loosing" were slang expressions of the rabbis. "To bind" meant to prohibit. "To loose" meant to permit. This use represented legislative power. In the circle of rabbis, "to bind" also meant to declare liable. "To loose" also meant to declare free. This use represented judicial power. By the first of these they "bound" or "loosed" acts or things; by the second they "remitted" or "retained," declared a person free from or liable to punishment, to compensation, or to sacrifice.

What does it mean for the church to have the keys to God's kingdom? Offer specific examples.

How do you feel about the responsibility Jesus gave to his disciples?

These powers—the legislative and the judicial—Jesus gave to Peter as the representative of the apostles. These powers, given to Peter here, Jesus also gave to the other apostles later. Jesus told the disciples, "Truly I tell you, whatever you bind on earth will be bound in heaven, and whatever you loose on earth will be loosed in heaven" (Matthew 18:18). After the Resurrection, Jesus said to the apostles, "Receive the Holy Spirit. If you forgive the sins of any, they are forgiven them; if you retain the sins of any, they are retained" (John 20:22-23). Under the guidance of the Holy Spirit, whatever the apostles bound or loosed on earth would be bound or loosed in heaven.

Who Is Jesus?

Jesus asked his disciples, " 'Who do people say that I am?' And they answered him, 'John the Baptist; and others, Elijah; and still others, one of the prophets.'...'But who do you

Who Is Jesus? ■

Review the core Bible passages mentioned at the beginning of the session. Write two or three sentences summarizing what you believe about Jesus.

"The Messiah, the Son of the Living God" ■

The Messiah is the one chosen by God to usher in God's kingdom. The kingdom of God is not heaven. Use a Bible dictionary to learn more about the kingdom of heaven and the kingdom of God.

say that I am?' Peter answered him, 'You are the Messiah.' "

It's a good question. Who is Jesus? People offer various opinions. "I try to follow Jesus' teachings in my life." "I think of Jesus as the Good Shepherd, taking care of us like lost lambs." "Jesus was a rebel. He questioned the politicians, the religious establishment." "Jesus works miracles; he heals people if they have faith." "If you follow Jesus, he'll change your life." "Every day is the Lord's day." "Jesus is—well—Jesus loves me." All of us have ideas about Jesus.

Of course, we also have the benefit of doctrine: "Jesus is our Lord and Savior." "Jesus died for our sins." But do we have any idea what the doctrine means? Children, during the children's sermon, answer "God" or "Jesus" in response to every question. Like them, we know the right answers, even though we may not have heard the question or understood the answer. The truth is that sometimes we are pretty confused about Jesus.

"The Messiah, the Son of the Living God"

"But who do you say that I am?" asks Jesus. Peter answers, "You are the Messiah." (In Matthew 16:16, "You are the Messiah, the Son of the living God"; in Luke 9:20, "The Messiah of God.") Peter has the right answer. Jesus is the Messiah, the one chosen by God to usher in God's kingdom.

God's kingdom is a new covenant and a new social order:

See, the home of God is among mortals.
He will dwell with them;
they will be his peoples,
and God himself will be with them;
he will wipe every tear from their eyes.

Read these Scripture passages to find out more about God's kingdom, which is often described as a restored Jerusalem.

Psalm 145:10-13
Isaiah 9:6-7
Isaiah 61:1-4
Isaiah 65:17-25
Micah 4:1-4
Zephaniah 3:14-20
Matthew 5:1-12

Death will be no more;
mourning and crying and pain will be no more.

Revelation 21:3-4

In Matthew, John sends word to Jesus, asking if he is, in fact, the Messiah. Jesus answers, "Go and tell John what you hear and see: the blind receive their sight, the lame walk, the lepers are cleansed, the deaf hear, the dead are raised, and the poor have good news brought to them" (Matthew 11:4-5). Jesus tells them, 'see for yourselves. The kingdom of God is happening before your eyes."

Peter confesses, "You are the Messiah." Yes.

Foundation in Faith ■

Peter was the first of the new people of God. Yet Peter's faith was no more or less than our own. Jesus promises to build the church on the fact of God's kingdom.

Consider: In what ways do you, as a community of faith, reflect Peter's faith in Jesus as the Messiah?

In what ways is your church built on the foundation of God's kingdom?

Foundation in Faith

In Mark and in Luke, Jesus responds to Peter by ordering him and the disciples to tell no one. In Matthew, Jesus says to Peter, "Blessed are you.... For flesh and blood has not revealed this to you, but my Father in heaven" (Matthew 16:17). Jesus says that Peter's faith is a revelation from God. The verse sounds like one of the beatitudes, "Blessed are ... for...." Peter is blessed by God's revelation. Faith is a gift.

Jesus continues, "You are Peter, and on this rock I will build my church" (Matthew 16:18). Jesus will build on Peter, the first among the new people of God and the starting point for gathering God's people into communities of faith. Jesus will also build on Peter's confession, adding structure and dimension to the foundation of faith: "You are the Messiah." Jesus will bring in God's kingdom, on which the church is built.

Keys and Binding and Loosing

What are the keys to the kingdom? What does it mean to bind and to loose?

Jesus gives to Peter the keys to the king-

Keys and Binding and Loosing ■

Draw an outline of a church. Write on the inside of the outline the names of people or groups of people who are welcome in your church. Write on the outside of the outline the names of people or groups of people who, for a variety of reasons, are excluded from the church.

dom and says to the disciples, "Whatever you bind on earth will be bound in heaven, and whatever you loose on earth will be loosed in heaven" (Matthew 16:19). John 20:23 may explain further: "If you forgive the sins of any, they are forgiven them; if you retain the sins of any, they are retained."

Some suggest that the Scripture is reminiscent of Isaiah 22:20-22, in which God gives to Eliakim "the key of the house of David; he shall open, and no one shall shut; he shall shut, and no one shall open." God gave to Eliakim the power to allow entrance to the palace and access to the king. If the reference is true, then the disciples were given the power under the guidance of the Holy Spirit to allow or to prohibit entrance to God's kingdom and access to God.

Does the Scripture imply that the church is given the keys to the kingdom? Perhaps. Are people who are included in the church also welcome in God's kingdom? Are people who are excluded or excommunicated from the church prohibited from entering the Kingdom? The Scripture seems to say so.

Discuss: Who should be included in the church? in God's kingdom? Who does Jesus include? exclude?

We must not, however, forget about the guidance of the Holy Spirit. The keys may be given to Peter and the disciples for "binding" and "loosing," but the Kingdom is God's. As fragile and sinful creatures along with the rest of humankind, the disciples knew that without the guidance of the Spirit and the grace of God in matters of inclusion and exclusion, they may never be admitted to the Kingdom. Being a disciple of Christ means accepting incredible responsibility! It also means demonstrating an amazing grace.

What responsibility do you have as a disciple to address the issue of inclusion and exclusion in the church?

So What?

We are not always clear about who Jesus is. Faith is a gift.

So What? ■

Describe Peter's relationship to Jesus.

How has learning about Peter helped to answer your questions about discipleship?

Jesus heralds the beginning of God's kingdom, in which the blind see, the lame walk, the dead are raised, and the poor hear the good news. To be a Christian disciple means to confess, with Peter, that Jesus is the Messiah, who will bring in the kingdom of God.

Jesus builds the church on Peter, who is the first of the new people of God. The church is founded on God's kingdom, and the disciples are given the keys.

Confessing Jesus as Messiah equals living for the kingdom. Consider: How do we, as disciples of Christ, preach good news to the poor? How do we witness to the Resurrection or give sight to the blind?

Jesus gives his disciples the keys. We have the power to decide who's in and who's out of God's kingdom. The issues churches struggle with today relate to who should be included and who should be excluded from the community. Churches are making decisions: Should homosexuals be ordained? Should unrepentant sinners be allowed in the door? Should we lock church doors against theft and keep the homeless from sleeping on church pews? Are the same people welcome in Sunday worship and the Wednesday lunch for the poor? Jesus expects us to make our churches look like God's kingdom. So the real question is, Who's in and who's out of the Kingdom?

Perhaps disciples of Christ should learn, with Peter, that followers of Jesus forgive "not seven times, but seventy-seven times" (Matthew 18:22) and that the doors to God's kingdom are wide open.

Prayer ■

God, you sent Jesus to bring in your kingdom. Remind us of his love and teach us to forgive in his name. Amen.

Session Four

Discipleship

Read Matthew 16:21-28; Mark 8:31—9:1; Luke 9:21-27.

Session Focus ■

This session deals with Jesus' announcement that the Son of Man must suffer and die, with Peter's response, and with our own feelings about Jesus' death. It also looks at the meaning of self-denial.

Session Objective ■

To face the suffering and death of Jesus and to look at our lives in light of Jesus' teaching: "Those who want to save their life will lose it, and those who lose their life for my sake, and for the sake of the gospel, will save it" (Mark 8:35).

Session Preparation ■

Read the Scripture. Read through the material in this chapter. Have available copies of a daily newspaper. Obtain a copy of *The Life of Jesus*, by Frederick Buechner, with photographs by Lee Boltin (Weathervane Books, 1974) or another book of religious art.

At Caesarea Philippi Peter recognized and acknowledged Jesus to be the Christ, the Messiah, the Son of the living God. Jesus commended Peter for this confession. Then Jesus began to tell the disciples what their belief would involve. They needed to know Jesus as the Messiah and to know the true nature of his Messiahship.

At the time of Jesus, several different expectations about the Messiah were current.

Messianic Expectations

Daniel 7 reports a vision in which Daniel saw four beasts come up out of the sea successively. These four beasts represented four kings who would rise to power and dominate the world. Finally the Ancient of Days (God) ascended to the throne. And with the clouds of heaven one like a human being, a son of man, came to the Ancient of Days and was presented before the throne. To this one like a son of man was given everlasting "dominion and glory and kingship, / that all peoples, nations, and languages / should serve him" (Daniel 7:14). This vision became a source of Jewish messianic expectations and "son of man" became a messianic title.

In some Jewish literature around the time of Jesus, "son of man" was used to refer to the

Messianic ■
Expectations

Complete these sentences:

The one God raises up to rule the earth is like a

When I picture Jesus' Second Coming, I see

When I remember the stories of Jesus, I think of

In my life, I experience the risen Christ as

Ask: In what ways are our pictures of the Messiah like Jewish expectations? How are they different?

messiah. They sought to supply in their own ways what Daniel had left untold about this one like a son of man. In John 12:34, in response to Jesus' statement, the Jewish people said, "We have heard from the law that the Messiah remains forever. How can you say that the Son of Man must be lifted up?" In this statement, the Jewish people equated the son of man with the messiah. According to this line of messianic expectation, the messiah would appear at the end of the age and would rule over the whole world forever. All of these events would take place supernaturally.

Another line of messianic expectation was popular among the Jews at that time. This idea was very nationalistic. About six centuries before the time of Christ, the Jewish nation was destroyed and the people were taken into captivity to Babylonia. In order to preserve their faith in the environment of a foreign culture, they established the institution of the synagogue. However, the genius of Jewish religion could not rest in this division of "sacred" and "secular." The ideals taught in the synagogue must be realized in the national life. The unity of the political and spiritual life of Israel that was broken at the time of the destruction of the nation had to be restored.

To the Jewish religious faith, obeying the God-given law of Moses and participating in the divinely ordained ritual of the Temple were very essential. These were also Israel's unbreakable link with the past, giving the Jews the sense of God's election. However, under foreign domination Jews were not free to obey the ancient law and to observe the rituals.

The Suffering Messiah

In their struggle for national independence, the Jews awaited the coming of the

The Suffering Messiah

Read Luke 24:44-49 and Acts 1:3-8. What was the expectation of a messiah? What would he do and for whom? How is the Messiah or Son of Man universal?

messiah, a son of David. This messiah would purify Jerusalem, destroy the ungodly nations, and convict the sinners, they believed. He would give the earth to Israel and free the Jews from the heathen in their midst. He would set up a righteous kingdom. This messianic expectation was accepted by the great mass of people.

The disciples of Jesus also shared this messianic expectation. After Jesus' resurrection, two disciples on their way to Emmaus told the "stranger" with whom they walked, "But we had hoped that he was the one to redeem Israel" (Luke 24:21). Before the Ascension, the disciples asked Jesus, "Lord, is this the time when you will restore the kingdom to Israel?" (Acts 1:6).

Merely recognizing Jesus as the Messiah is not enough. After Peter's confession, Jesus "began to teach them that the Son of Man must undergo great suffering, and be rejected by the elders, the chief priests, and the scribes, and be killed, and after three days rise again" (Mark 8:31).

Use a Bible dictionary to look up "Son of Man." What does it mean? When and where is it used in the Bible?

Since the title *messiah* had so many meanings to the public as well as in the minds of the disciples, Jesus preferred to use the title the *Son of Man* instead. As pointed out earlier, the son of man was a messianic title. Significantly, Jesus did not use "son of man" or "a son of man." When Jesus used this title, it was always definite, "*the* Son of Man." This means Jesus was always referring to the well-known figure. That figure is the one like a son of man who came with the clouds of heaven to the Ancient of Days in Daniel 7:13.

This Son of Man would have dominion, glory, and kingship. All peoples, nations, and languages would serve him. The whole scene in Daniel 7 was supernatural. The coming of this Son of Man was with the clouds of heaven, which were a symbol of a theophany (appearing of God). Therefore, we are not correct to think that when Jesus used the title *the Son of Man* he meant to emphasize his humanity. The perspective of Daniel 7 is universalistic, including all peoples, nations, and languages. This fits into Jesus' messianic ministry much better than the title *messiah*, which had a strong nationalistic emphasis in the mind of the Jews.

Since, in the minds of the Jews, the title *messiah* was closely connected with kingship, the Jews had difficulty accepting the idea of a suffering messiah. So Jesus hesitated to use the title *messiah* before his passion. However after his passion and resurrection, this problem was no more. After the Resurrection, Jesus used "the Christ" or "the Messiah" more freely. He told the two disciples on the way to Emmaus, "Was it not necessary that the Messiah should suffer these things and then enter into his glory?" (Luke 24:26). Again he told the two disciples, "Thus it is written, that the Messiah is to suffer and to rise from the dead on the third day" (Luke 24:46).

After Peter's confession, Jesus began to teach the disciples that even though he was the Son of Man he must suffer and die. He must, because that was God's will. That was God's plan for his messianic mission. At this, Peter began to rebuke Jesus. For Peter, messiahship excluded suffering and death. Jesus immediately recognized Satan's temptation in this rebuke. Earlier in the wilderness Satan had tempted Jesus by offering him the kingdom of the world without the cross. Both times Jesus told Satan to be gone (Matthew 4:8-10; Mark 8:33). He chose to obey God's will even if obedience meant suffering and the cross.

Jesus said that the Son of God must suffer and die. Read Isaiah 53.

Would you ordinarily associate with the Messiah these words from the Scripture? Why? Why not?
despised
rejected
infirmity
no account
stricken
bruised
oppressed
death

In doing this, Peter did not set his mind on the things of God, but the things of human beings (Matthew 16:23; Mark 8:33). To set one's mind on that thing with moral interest is to let that thing determine one's basic attitude of life. That thing on which one sets one's mind surely will have the highest moral value for that person.

Peter did not understand true discipleship. So Jesus gave him and others an important lesson on it in Mark 8:34-38.

Self-Denial

Self-Denial ■

Read Mark 8:34-38 and Matthew 10:37-39. What, do you think, did Jesus mean when he spoke about loving mother or father more than him? about losing and finding life?

True discipleship involves denying oneself. Contrary to what Peter did here, the true disciple should set his or her mind (in the sense explained earlier) on the things of God, not those of others or of oneself. Mark 8:35 indicates that the ultimate goal of denying oneself is to save one's life. Therefore to deny oneself does not mean to ignore, or to be unconcerned, about oneself.

Jesus made a similar statement in Matthew 10:37, 39. "Whoever loves father or mother more than me is not worthy of me." Those who find their life will lose it, and those who lose their life for my sake will find it." In the light of Matthew 10:37-39, to deny oneself means to love Jesus more than oneself.

What does it mean to deny yourself? What does it mean to take up our cross and follow Jesus? to take it daily? What examples can you cite of doing something "for the sake of" Jesus?

When one's own interest comes into conflict with that of Jesus, the true disciple will put the latter above the former.

The true disciple should find the way of the Master and follow him. Jesus' way was that of the cross. The true disciple should take up his or her cross and follow Jesus. This does not mean, however, that the disciples should be crucified physically, though many were. Luke reports that followers were to "take up their cross daily" (Luke 9:23). The crucifixion of the disciples is metaphorical

What does it mean to "be ashamed of me [Jesus]"? What examples can you cite? What are the consequences?

rather than actual. Disciples should be willing to sacrifice themselves, even to die, for the sake of Jesus and his gospel. They should follow Jesus and be loyal to him even unto death, if that extreme becomes necessary.

"Those who are ashamed of me and of my words in this adulterous and sinful generation, of them the Son of Man will also be ashamed when he comes in the glory of his Father with the holy angels" (Mark 8:38). Here is the glorious scene of the Son of Man as shown in Daniel 7. What one does today with regard to Jesus will determine what one's rewards will be when Jesus returns in his glory.

God's Kingdom Come? ■

Read the morning paper. Cut out headlines, photographs, and articles. How many can you find that support the idea that God's kingdom has come? How many support the idea that God's kingdom has not come?

How do we balance the faith statement that the Kingdom *has* come, but *will* come?

God's Kingdom Come?

Sometimes it's hard to believe in Jesus. Jesus proclaims God's kingdom come, where there will be no crying or pain, where the blind see and the lame walk and death is no more. But clearly God's kingdom has not come.

Read the headlines in the daily paper: *Crisis in the Middle East Escalates, Homicide Rate Highest Ever, Public Officials in Fund Raising Scam, E-Coli Epidemic, Thousands Homeless After Earthquake, Children Starving in Asia.* We do not have to look too far to see that God's kingdom has not come.

Still, we believe. We look for life after death, when God will reward the good and punish the wicked. We hope for the continuation of our souls, for a better life "in the sweet by and by." If we keep our eyes on Jesus, there will be room for us in God's mansion. Christian faith has become a cloudy hope for personal salvation.

On the other hand, Christian faith is sure knowledge that Jesus will win the victory against sin and death and will come again in clouds of angelic splendor. In the struggle between good and evil, Jesus will ultimately triumph. If we hold fast to Jesus, standing our ground on issues of personal morality, we will celebrate the victory with him.

Even if we cannot confess that Jesus is Messiah or that God's kingdom has come, we're still faithful. Like Peter, we believe in Jesus.

Suffering and Death ■
Look at a variety of pictures of the Crucifixion. If possible, use *The Life of Jesus*, by Frederick Buechner. Ask: Which pictures are most like your idea of the Crucifixion?

If the Crucifixion happened today, what do you think it would be like? Explain.

How do you feel about Jesus suffering and death?

Suffering and Death

Jesus answered Peter that "the Son of Man must undergo great suffering and be rejected by the elders, the chief priests, and the scribes, and be killed, and after three days rise again" (Mark 8:31).

Jesus suffered and died. He was arrested and tried and convicted on charges of blasphemy and treason. He didn't stand a chance in the courts of law.

The scene of his crucifixion was not unlike an American execution. Every hate group in Jerusalem probably showed up, and someone sold cold drinks and popcorn on the corner. If the press had recorded the crowd's responses, what would they have heard? "Serves him right." "What goes around comes around—you can't deny it." "If he's the Messiah, let him save himself." "I firmly believe that justice has been done today."

Jesus was left to die, dangling from a cross, stark against a darkening sky. Jesus, apparently forsaken, screamed at a God who seemed not to hear.

"But Jesus, You Don't Have to Die" ■
Jesus said that the Son of Man must suffer and die. Read Matthew 16:21.

"But Jesus, You Don't Have to Die"

We don't like it any better than Peter did. Peter responded to Jesus' announcement, "God forbid it, Lord! This must never happen to you" (Matthew 16:22). We might say something similar: "Jesus, you don't have to die. After all, saviors don't die!"

Jesus' suffering and death call our faith into question. How can a savior who died save us from death? How can Jesus, the victor, be so frail?

The Bible and the creeds of the church are clear that Jesus *died*: "We believe in Jesus who was crucified, dead, and buried" (The Apostles Creed). Yet, our inclination is to ignore Jesus' death. We skip from Palm Sunday to Easter. We try not to teach our children about Good Friday; it's just too gruesome. When we talk about salvation, we look to heavenly kingdoms and a risen Christ. When we talk about victory, we think of Jesus seated on a heavenly throne with all the nations at his feet. We do our best not to talk at all about Jesus strung up on a wooden cross.

We're a lot like Peter. We would rather not believe that Jesus suffered and died.

Discuss: What would our faith be like if we just skipped the "Good Friday part"?

Why did Jesus die? Why was he crucified? Would God plan for Jesus' suffering and death? If Jesus is God, why did he not save himself? Why couldn't Jesus bring in God's kingdom with glory and power and majesty?

Me? Satan?

Jesus' response to Peter is frightening: "Get behind me, Satan!" (Mark 8:33). Jesus must suffer and die. Peter, like Satan, tempts him to avoid death and save himself. Of course, we agree. Jesus doesn't need to die.

Me? Satan?

Have you unwittingly tempted Jesus Christ as Peter did? Describe the experience and the consequences.

Deny Yourself and Follow Me

Peter set his mind not on divine things, but on human things. In contrast, Jesus calls his followers to "deny themselves and take up their cross and follow me." For those who want to save their life will lose it, and those who lose their life for my sake, and for the sake of the gospel, will save it" (Mark 8:34-35).

Jesus denied himself and lost his life for the sake of the good news: God's kingdom. He was crucified because he was the Messiah. What does Jesus ask of his disciples?

Deny Yourself and Follow Me

Reflect: In what ways is your life defined by death?

A young theologian said, "Don't you see that we can't do without death? Who we are is defined by how we deal with dying." She's right, of course. Knowing we're going to die, we try to find meaning in wealth or social status. We try to make a difference. We get involved in education or art. Catching sight of the yawning emptiness of death, we fill our days with too much to do. We run away in business. Setting our minds on human things is being defined by death.

How would your life change if you set your mind on divine things? In what specific ways can you begin to live for God's kingdom?

What would happen if we gave it all up and faced death head on? What if we were willing to lose our lives, to follow Jesus to the cross and die with him? Giving up the mad scramble to avoid death, we could live. Perhaps we could begin to set our minds on divine things, and we could live for God's kingdom, which is life.

So What?

Peter's relationship with Jesus teaches us about Christian discipleship. Our faith, like Peter's, wavers in the face of Jesus' suffering and death. Being a disciple means facing death—both his and our own. It means following Jesus right up to the cross if need be.

Discipleship means losing our lives as they are and living instead for the sake of the good news: the kingdom of God. So—what does it mean to set our minds on divine things?

So What? ■

Describe Peter's relationship to Jesus.

How has learning about Peter helped to answer your questions about discipleship?

Prayer ■

God, take us to the cross. Lead us to deny ourselves for the sake of your kingdom, and give us life in your Son, Jesus Christ. Amen.

Session Five

The Transfiguration

Read Matthew 16:28—17:13; Mark 9:1-13; Luke 9:27-36.

Session Focus ■
This session puts in juxta-position Jesus' transfigura-tion, in which he was glori-fied as the Messiah, and his ministry, which finally led to the cross.

Session Objective ■
To realize that disciples of Christ follow Jesus to the mountaintop, where Jesus is glorified, and into the valleys, where people cry out for healing.

Session Preparation ■
Read the Scriptures. Read through the material in this chapter. Have available paper, felt-tip markers, and pictures of the Crucifixion from Session 4.

Session Outline ■
Choose from among these activities and discussion questions.

After Peter's great confession at Caesarea Philippi, Jesus disclosed to the disciples his upcoming suffering, death, and resurrection. Peter objected to this announcement. Surely the other disciples also must have been per-plexed. Jesus' short discourse on true disci-pleship probably did not calm their bewilder-ment.

While the apostles were still puzzled, Jesus took Peter, James, and John and led them onto a high mountain. When Jesus began to pray, the appearance of his countenance changed and his garment became dazzling white. The glory that was concealed in Jesus and would be fully revealed at his Second Coming became temporarily evident.

Jesus: An Act of Salvation

Then Moses and Elijah appeared and talked with Jesus about his departure (Luke 9:31). The Greek word translated "depar-ture" here is *exodus*, exactly the same word as the English *exodus*. The topic of conversation among Jesus, Moses, and Elijah was Jesus' exodus. This may have meant simply the death of Jesus, or it may have meant the whole event of Jesus' death, resurrection, and ascension as his departure to heaven. This whole event signifies the death of Jesus as an

Jesus: An Act of Salvation ■

Read Malachi 4:4–5.

Malachi tells the people to remember the covenant with Moses and to look for Elijah, who will bring harmony before the day of the Lord. The day of the Lord is the day when God's reign is established.

Now read Matthew 16:28–17:13. What is the relationship among Moses, Elijah, and Jesus? How did Peter respond to Jesus' transfiguration? If you had been in Peter's place, how would you have responded?

act of salvation, repeating the Exodus from Egypt under the leadership of Moses. Whatever the precise meaning of the word *exodus* here, it has to do with Jesus' death.

The three disciples were startled to see this glorious scene. Peter said to Jesus, "Rabbi, it is good for us to be here; let us make three dwellings, one for you, one for Moses, and one for Elijah" (Mark 9:5). Mark comments that Peter did not know what to say, for the apostles were exceedingly afraid.

In this statement we see some character features of Peter. Even though he did not know what to say, he felt he had to say something. He might have been better off not saying anything then. Earlier he had objected to Jesus' prediction of suffering and death. In sight of the cross Peter said, "God forbid it, Lord! This must never happen to you" (Matthew 16:22). In the light of glory Peter said, "Lord, it is good for us to be here" (Matthew 17:4). The cross? No. The glory? Yes.

Peter proposed to build three dwellings or booths, one each for Jesus, Moses, and Elijah. He contemplated treating Jesus, Moses, and Elijah as equals. This was not consistent with his great confession about a week before when he recognized Jesus as the Christ, the Son of the living God.

A Sign of God's Kingdom ■

How do you think what Peter, James, and John did with Jesus at the Transfiguration are indicators of how they would be during the rest of Jesus' ministry? after the Crucifixion?

A Sign of God's Kingdom

Suddenly a cloud overshadowed Jesus, Moses, and Elijah, and a voice from out of the cloud said, "This is my Son, the Beloved; with him I am well pleased; listen to him!" (Matthew 17:5). Then the disciples no longer saw anyone with them but Jesus only.

The whole scene of the Transfiguration was oriented toward the disciples. Jesus was "transfigured *before them*" (Mark 9:2, italics added).

How do you interpret the prophecy of Mark 9:1? Use a Bible commentary for further insight.

How do you imagine the Second Coming? What will the coming of God's kingdom be like?

Make a sign. Draw a picture and write words that describe the establishment of God's kingdom on earth. If you need help getting started, read Mark 13:24-27 or Revelation 21:1-4.

"There appeared *to them* Elijah with Moses" (Mark 9:4, italics added). "They saw no one *with them* any more, but only Jesus" (Mark 9:8, italics added). The Transfiguration was for the edification of the disciples.

Jesus' short discourse on true discipleship taught that what a person would do with Jesus in this present age would determine how Jesus would treat him or her at the glorious Second Coming. As a guarantee that the Son of Man would surely come in the glory of his Father with the holy angels, Jesus gave a sign to the disciples. "Truly, I tell you, there are some standing here who will not taste death until they see that the kingdom of God has come with power" (Mark 9:1).

Mark 9:2 reads, "Six days later, Jesus took with him Peter and James and John, and led them up a high mountain apart, by themselves. And he was transfigured before them." Mark seldom specifies the chronological relationship between the events he reports in the Gospel. Yet here he departs from his usual practice and specifies that the Transfiguration took place six days after Jesus' statement in the preceding verse, Mark 9:1. This seems to be the coming of the kingdom of God with power that is mentioned in Mark 9:1.

In the Gospels the kingdom of God and the person of Jesus are inseparably joined together. Matthew 19:29 reports Jesus as saying, "And everyone who has left houses or brothers or sisters or father or mother or children or fields, *for my name's sake*, will receive a hundredfold, and will inherit eternal life" (italics added). The same saying of Jesus is reported in Mark 10:29-30 as "Truly I tell you, there is no one who has left house or brothers or sisters or mother or father or children or fields, *for my sake and for the sake of the good news*, who will not receive a hundredfold . . . and in the age to come eternal life" (italics added). Luke 18:29-30 reports the same statement this way: "Truly I tell you, there is no one who has left house or wife or brothers or parents or children, *for the sake of the kingdom of God*, who will not get back very much more in this age, and in the age to come eternal life" (italics added). In other words, the expressions "for Jesus' sake," "for the sake of the gospel," "for the sake of the kingdom of God" all have the same meaning in this teaching of Jesus.

At the end of the short discourse on true discipleship, according to Matthew 16:28, Jesus said, "Truly I tell you, there are some standing here who will not taste death before they see *the Son of Man coming in his kingdom*" (italics added). Mark 9:1 reports Jesus as saying, "Truly, I tell you, there are some standing here who will not taste death until they see that *the kingdom of God has come with power*" (italics added). According to Luke 9:27, Jesus said, "But truly I tell you, there are some standing here who will not taste death before they see the *kingdom of God*" (italics added). Therefore the coming of the kingdom of God with power means the Son of Man coming in his kingdom.

Discuss: In what ways does the Transfiguration foreshadow the coming of God's kingdom?

The kingdom of God came when Jesus came to the earth and assaulted the kingdom of Satan to set persons free. Jesus declared, "But if it is by the Spirit of God that I cast out demons, then the kingdom of God has come to you" (Matthew 12:28). However, the consummation of the kingdom of God will come only when Jesus, the Son of Man, returns "in clouds with great power and glory" (Mark 13:26) and sits on the throne (Matthew 25:31). That is the time when the kingdom of God will come with power.

On the mountain of Transfiguration Jesus displayed the future glory of the Son of Man as a foreshadowing of his sure return in glory. Surely Peter understood the Transfiguration in this light (see 2 Peter 1:16-18).

Approval: "This Is My Son, the Beloved"

In the Transfiguration, Moses and Elijah appeared and talked with Jesus about his death. These two men were among the most remarkable in the Old Testament. Moses stood at the holy mountain representing the Law. Elijah represented the Prophets. The Law and the Prophets, that is, the entire Old Testament, rendered confirmation to Jesus' prediction of his own suffering and death.

While Peter was still offering to build dwellings, a cloud overshadowed Jesus and the two heavenly visitors. The cloud represented God's presence. And a voice from the cloud said, "This is my Son, the Beloved; with him I am well pleased; listen to him!" (Matthew 17:5). God intervened in Peter's blunder but confirmed his earlier great confession. Yes, this Jesus is the unique Son of God. Jesus predicted his suffering and death. This bewildered the disciples, yet God endorsed it. Jesus was right. They should listen to and obey him.

At the time of Jesus' baptism, a voice came from heaven saying, "This is my Son, the Beloved, with whom I am well pleased" (Matthew 3:17). At the end of Jesus' private life and the beginning of his public ministry God set the divine seal of approval upon Jesus' life. Toward the end of Jesus' public ministry, when he took the definite steps to go to Jerusalem to be crucified, God again set the

Approval: "This Is My Son, the Beloved"

Moses, Elijah, and Jesus talked about Jesus' death. God announced his approval: "This is my Son, the Beloved; listen to him!" (Mark 9:7). And Jesus said, "The Son of Man is about to suffer" (Matthew 17:12).

On the surface, the Transfiguration is about Jesus' glory. Below the surface, it's about Jesus' suffering. Put your picture side by side with a picture of the Crucifixion. Discuss: In what ways is Jesus' death an act of salvation? In what ways is it a sign of God's kingdom?

Twice in Scripture God appears to proclaim Jesus as the beloved Son. What do you think that means? What do you think the impact was on those who heard the announcement? How do you think you would feel to hear such a thing? What does it mean to listen to Jesus as the Son of God? Do you listen well?

seal of approval on Jesus' life and ministry.

The phrase "with whom I am well pleased" may refer to Isaiah 42:1. If this is the case, then both at the beginning and toward the end of Jesus' ministry God identified Jesus as the servant of the Lord. According to Isaiah 53, this servant of the Lord would suffer and die for the sins of many in order to be their redeemer. Even if the phrase "with whom I am well pleased" is not a reference to Isaiah 42:1, God still endorsed Jesus' decision to suffer and die. The voice from the cloud told the disciples to listen to Jesus because he had divine authority as the Son of God.

The Glory? Yes

Jesus is like Moses. In Jesus Christ, God establishes a new covenant with God's people. In Jesus' death, the kingdom of God has come.

The Glory? Yes

When we read about mountains in the Bible, we should be ready for God to make an appearance. Moses met God at the mountain (Exodus 3:1). Later God appeared in clouds and thunder at Mount Sinai to give the people of Israel the law (Exodus 19:16—20:18). Elijah went to the mountain to look for the Lord and heard God's voice in the "sound of sheer silence" (1 Kings 19:11-13). The mountain of the Lord is a symbol of God's kingdom. Isaiah 2:2-4 says that the mountain of the Lord will be raised up "in days to come" and all people and nations will come to the mountain to learn the ways of God and to become one people of God. Zechariah 8:3 promises that "the mountain of the Lord of hosts shall be called the holy mountain." The story of the Transfiguration begins "Jesus took with him Peter and James and his brother John and led them up a high mountain" (Matthew 17:1). Get ready for the presence of God and for a sign of God's kingdom.

Jesus was transformed. Suddenly "his

clothes became dazzling white" (Matthew 17:2). Mark 9:3 says as white "as no one on earth could bleach them." Clearly, Jesus' transfiguration was an act of God. Matthew 17:2 adds that "his face shone like the sun." When Moses came down from Mount Sinai, carrying the tablets of the law "the skin of his face shone because he had been talking with God" (Exodus 34:29). Matthew wants us to know that the Transfiguration is an act of God and a new covenant. God made a covenant with the people through Moses; God makes a new covenant with the people through Jesus Christ.

Moses and Elijah appeared and talked with Jesus. Moses represented the covenant at Sinai. Elijah was expected to return to herald God's kingdom. The presence of Moses, Elijah, and Jesus makes it clear: The kingdom of God has come near. In Jesus' death, his *exodus*, God has made a new covenant with God's people.

Build a Building

We react to the Transfiguration as Peter did. "Wow! Look at that—and to think we could have missed it!" And then we build buildings. In the face of the glory of God, we have no idea what we should do. So we build buildings—churches, cathedrals, education wings—trying to capture the majesty of the Lord.

Of course, buildings or dwellings aren't exactly a new idea. Read 2 Samuel 7:1-16. David wanted to build God a house. God, bemused, made a covenant with David: I will "make you a house, . . . I will raise up your offspring after you, . . . and I will establish the throne of [your] kingdom forever."

Peter, in his excitement, wanted to build a house for God. God was not as tolerant with

---

Reflect on times when you have experienced the presence of God. Has God come to you with power and glory? Have you realized the presence of God in times of trouble?

Do you recognize yourself as a partner in a covenant with God? What are your responsibilities and benefits in that covenant?

Build a Building ■

The Scripture reminds us of God's covenant with David. Read 2 Samuel 7:1-16.

Describe the building in which you worship. In what ways is it a holy place for you? How much of your church's budget is earmarked for buildings? Is your church involved in a building drive?

Roleplay a conversation between the building committee and God. Begin with the following dialogue:

COMMITTEE CHAIR: The administrative board has given us the task of making decisions about the new building.

COMMITTEE MEMBER: This building is falling down. It doesn't feel like we're going to church anymore.

GOD: Jesus is my Son, the Beloved. Listen to him.

Peter. A cloud covered the mountain; and a voice rumbled from the cloud, "This is my son, the Beloved; with him I am well pleased; listen to him!"

God's voice put a stop to Peter's flailing enthusiasm. Peter and the disciples "fell to the ground and were overcome by fear" (Matthew 17:6).

The cloud and the voice like thunder are reminiscent of God's covenant at Mount Sinai. The Transfiguration marks a new covenant. God's announcement lets us know that Jesus is, in fact, the son of God and the son of David (David means *Beloved*), the one whose kingdom will be established forever.

The Way to Jerusalem ■

Following Jesus means seeing the glory of God and knowing that God has established the new covenant in Jesus Christ.

Following Jesus also means being involved in his ministry. How do the post-Transfiguration events reflect our own day? Are we ever so bedazzled by the glow of a spiritual high that we neglect the suffering "at the foot of the mountain"? Explain.

Discuss: In what ways are you involved in the ministry of Jesus to the sick, the poor, the imprisoned, and the oppressed? How is your church involved in teaching and healing?

How do you understand your ministry in light of God's kingdom? What does it mean to follow Jesus to the cross?

The Way to Jerusalem

When Peter and the disciples got up and looked around, all they saw was Jesus. "Listen," God commanded. Listen to the word of the Lord: God's kingdom has come in Jesus. God has made a new covenant with God's people. You have seen God's glory. But the Son of Man "is to go through many sufferings and be treated with contempt" (Mark 9:12). The journey to the cross begins as Peter and the disciples follow Jesus down the mountain.

When they arrive at the foot of the mountain, a crowd of people runs to meet them. A man explains: I brought my son, who has seizures, but your disciples could not heal him.

Jesus, clearly annoyed, condemns the crowd and the disciples: "You faithless and perverse generation" (Matthew 17:17). Then he heals the boy.

Jesus condemns the present age, our age, in which children suffer and religious people look on, with no idea of what to do. And he also signals the coming age, God's kingdom, in which children are well and the religious are blessed with faith.

So What? ■

Describe Peter's relationship to Jesus.

How has learning about Peter helped to answer your questions about discipleship?

Prayer ■

God, show us your love in the triumph and in the suffering of Jesus Christ. Amen.

So What?

The Transfiguration has all the razzle-dazzle of a Hollywood extravaganza: a spectacular transformation, all the stars in one place. It's what we've been waiting for. Actually, it's what we and generations of faithful people have been waiting for. The Transfiguration is a sign that God's kingdom will come and God's covenant will be restored.

What does Christian discipleship mean? It seems to mean that we do have mountaintop experiences, in which we are sure of God and God's promises. In our enthusiasm, we're apt to flail around with no clue of how we should respond. God does not seem to appreciate our propensity for building buildings.

Christian disciples follow Jesus up the mountain and then into the valleys, where people cry out for healing. Faith is not razzle-dazzle. It's the hard work of teaching and healing (proclaiming the good news of God's kingdom). Faith is following Jesus down the mountain and to the cross, where the Son of Man will suffer and die.

Session Six

Peter's Denial

Read Matthew 26:20-56, 69-75; Mark 14:17-72; Luke 22:14-71; John 13:1-38; 18:15-27.

Session Focus ■
This session looks more closely at Peter's faith and his denial of Jesus. It also considers our failure to be faithful and looks for salvation in the death and resurrection of Jesus Christ.

Session Objective ■
To realize that being a disciple of Christ does not mean being perfectly faithful. Instead discipleship is having a share in Christ and the new life he offers.

Session Preparation ■
Read the Scripture. Read through the material in this chapter.

Session Outline ■
Choose from among these activities and discussion questions.

After the Transfiguration, Jesus moved steadily to Jerusalem. Jesus, time and again, predicted his suffering and death at the hands of the religious leaders. He tried to prepare the disciples for the event.

Yet Jesus' prediction did not take the minds of the disciples off their ambitions. They wanted to know who would be greatest in the kingdom of God (Matthew 18:1; Mark 9:33-34; Luke 9:46). Then James and John requested that one of them sit at Jesus' right hand and the other at his left in his kingdom. The other disciples were indignant at them for making this request (Matthew 20:20-28; Mark 10:35-45).

In Luke and in John, the issue of greatness was raised during the Last Supper and might have been related to the way the disciples were positioned at the table. We do not have sufficient information to determine the exact seating at the table at the Last Supper. However, the host, the most important person, would have reclined in the center of a series of couches. The place of honor was to the left of the host. The second place was to the host's right. In John, this second place of honor was occupied by the disciple "whom Jesus loved," probably John (John 13:23). Peter was in a position where he could be seen easily by John, because he made a sign to John that was easily visible to John (John 13:24). So Peter was not in the place of honor on the left of Jesus; if he were, he would have asked Jesus himself instead of making a sign to John to ask Jesus.

Footwashing

In the Gospel of John, Jesus rose during the supper, laid aside his garment, and girded himself with a towel. Then he poured water into a basin and began to wash the feet of the disciples and to wipe them with the towel. When he came to Peter, Peter said, "Lord, are *you* going to wash *my* feet?" (John 13:6, italics added). In the Greek, "you" and "my" are both emphatic and placed in sharp contrast. Peter made a very strong emphatic statement. "You will never wash my feet" (John 13:8). Even though Jesus told Peter what he was doing, Peter did not understand at that moment.

Jesus answered him, "Unless I wash you, you have no share with me" (John 13:8).

Peter loved Jesus so much that he could not bear to think that he might not have a part in Jesus. So he said to Jesus, "Lord, not my feet only but also my hands and my head!" (John 13:9).

Jesus said to him, "One who has bathed does not need to wash, except for the feet, but is entirely clean. And you [plural] are clean, though not all of you" (John 13:10).

Who Me?

During the supper Jesus announced, "One of you will betray me." The disciples were very sorrowful and began to ask Jesus one after another, "Surely not I?" (Matthew 26:21-22; Mark 14:18-19). They were concerned lest they might unknowingly betray

Footwashing ■

Read aloud the following dialogue:

PETER: Are you going to wash my feet?
JESUS: You do not know now what I am doing, but later you will understand.
PETER: You will never wash my feet.
JESUS: Unless I wash you, you have no share with me.
PETER: Lord, not my feet only but also my hands and my head!
JESUS: One who has bathed does not need to wash, except for the feet, but is entirely clean. And you are clean.

Read John 13:3-15. Look up *footwashing* in a Bible dictionary or commentary. What is its significance in the biblical context?

Discuss: Peter is talking about washing feet. For Jesus, footwashing is a ritual. What does Jesus say about salvation? service?

Read John 12:1-7.

Discuss: What, do you think, is the relationship between Mary's anointing Jesus' feet (John 12:1-7) and footwashing (John 13:3-15)?

When Jesus said, "One of you will betray me," the disciples looked around at one another, saying, "Who me?" Who were the people involved in Jesus' death? Make a list. Add to the list people who fled for their lives or betrayed him or denied him. Add to the list people from history who have in some way betrayed Jesus.

Maybe we should all ask, "Who me?" Do you think it is possible to be perfectly faithful? To never betray or deny Jesus?

Jesus. Except for Judas, no one intended to betray Jesus. Peter was far away from Jesus, and he could not whisper to Jesus. He made a sign to John who was lying close to the breast of Jesus to find out about whom Jesus was speaking. Peter was anxious to know who the betrayer was. He might have been just curious. More probably, however, he was concerned that he might become the betrayer unknowingly. He wanted to be faithful.

After the supper Jesus told the disciples that they would all fall away because of him that night. Peter declared to him, "Though all become deserters because of you, I will never desert you" (Matthew 26:33). Peter was loyal. Jesus told him, "Truly I tell you, this very night, before the cock crows, you will deny me three times" (Matthew 26:34).

Peter could not believe this would ever happen. He protested, "Even though I must die with you, I will not deny you" (Matthew 26:35; see also Mark 14:27-31; Luke 22:31-34; and John 13:36-38).

What a contrast! When Jesus first announced his suffering and death after Peter's great confession at Caesarea Philippi, Peter objected. He did not want that for Jesus or for himself. But at this time he was ready to die with Jesus. He wanted to be faithful to Jesus even to death.

Denial and ■ Restoration

Read Mark 13:32-37. Jesus tells the disciples to stay awake and to watch for the coming of God's kingdom. Not long afterward, he asks them to stay awake in the garden of Gethsemane while he prays. But Peter and the other disciples are unable

Denial and Restoration

Luke gives us some spiritual insights into the situation. Jesus told Peter that Satan had demanded to have all the disciples that he might sift them like wheat. But Jesus had prayed for Peter that his faith might not fail. Jesus told Peter to strengthen his brethren after his return to the former spiritual condition (Luke 22:31-32). Satan was to assault all the disciples. Judas gave in totally. Jesus to stay awake even for a little while.

If the disciples are unable to stay awake and watch for God's kingdom, how can they have a share in the new life of Christ? What does it mean to "have a share"?

Though we claim to be faithful, we fail. How can we have a share in the new life? If we cannot be perfectly faithful, should we be concerned about these lapses? Explain.

Before the Cock Crowed ■

Read John 13:1-38; 18:15-27. Summarize everything that happened. Who did what? Why do you think each person acted or failed to act?

prayed especially for Peter. Jesus assigned to Peter the mission of strengthening his brethren.

After the Last Supper, Jesus took the apostles to the garden of Gethsemane. He left eight disciples near the entrance to the garden and took Peter, James, and John farther into the garden. He told the eight to sit and wait, but he told these three to watch and pray so that they would not enter into temptation (Matthew 26:41). They had made some lofty claims. Peter claimed that he would not deny Jesus even if he had to die with him. James and John earlier claimed that they would be able to drink the cup Jesus was to drink (Matthew 20:22; Mark 10:38-39). Jesus himself went a little farther to pray. When Jesus came back to see these three, they were in sound sleep. The spirit was willing, but the flesh was weak.

Late that night Judas led a crowd from the Jewish authorities to the garden of Gethsemane to arrest Jesus. In John, Peter tried to defend Jesus. He drew a sword and struck the high priest's slave, Malchus, and cut off his right ear (John 18:10). Jesus told Peter to put his sword into its sheath and healed Malchus's ear. Peter might have acted impetuously, but still his loyalty to Jesus and his courage prompted this action.

Before the Cock Crowed

In the Gospel of John, when Jesus was arrested, the disciples fled. Peter was concerned enough to follow Jesus, even though afar off, to the court of the high priest. Another disciple who was known to the high priest also did the same thing. We do not know for sure who this other disciple was. Some think it was Nicodemus or Joseph of Arimathea. An early tradition identifies him

Why would the Bible tell the story of Peter's denial?

as John, son of Zebedee. Whoever he was, since he was known to the high priest, it was safe for him to be in the court of the high priest. But it was not so for Peter. It took high loyalty and courage for Peter to appear there; it was risky. The other disciple could count on the high priest to get him out of trouble. But Peter did not have such protection. His action was like entering a lion's den.

So Peter stood outside at the door. When the other disciple saw this, he went out and asked the maid who was keeping the door to let Peter enter (John 18:15-16).

Inside the court of the high priest Peter was asked his relationship with Jesus. First, a maid of the high priest saw him and asked him. John specifies this maid as the one who was keeping the door when Peter entered. She said to him, "You are not also one of this man's disciples, are you?" (John 18:17).

To this question Peter answered, "I am not."

Peter warmed by the fire. A second time he was accused of being one of Jesus' disciples. Again he denied it.

Peter said, "I do not know him." Why do we consider Peter to be the model of discipleship?

How well, under the circumstances, do you think Peter acquitted himself as a disciple?

About one hour later, someone in the crowd insisted that Peter was one of Jesus' disciples; he had seen Peter with Jesus at the garden. Peter strongly denied his knowledge of Jesus. At this moment the cock crowed. In Luke, Jesus turned and looked at Peter (Luke 22:61). Peter recalled Jesus' prediction of his denial and went out and wept bitterly.

Throughout this night of betrayal Peter wanted to be loyal to the Master. Out of his real love for Jesus Peter wanted Jesus to wash him thoroughly. Because of his deep loyalty to Jesus he pledged that he would die with Jesus if necessary. In genuine concern for Jesus, he drew the sword to protect the Master. Because of his faithfulness, Peter alone followed Jesus to the lion's den, while the rest of the disciples fled for their own safety. True, he cracked under the pressure. However, beneath the failure was this deep loyalty and genuine love.

Peter's Faith

Peter's Faith ▮

Write a want ad for the perfect disciple.

Decide: Does Peter qualify? Why? Why not? How would you respond to the question in this section's last paragraph?

Peter's faith was not extraordinary. Peter wasn't a scholar; he simply didn't understand Jesus. He wasn't especially courageous. Peter threw himself into discipleship with bungling enthusiasm (a kind of bull-in-a-china-shop faith). But when his faith was tested, he wavered. No, he caved in. When questioned, "You also were with Jesus the Galilean," he answered, straight out, "I do not know what you are talking about" (Matthew 26:69-70).

Peter's faith was not extraordinary, but he is a model of discipleship. The question is, Why? It seems that being a disciple is following Jesus, no matter what. It's finding a spiritual center for our lives, discerning God's will, and being obedient. Shouldn't disciples stand their ground in faith and morals? Shouldn't they at least own up to knowing Jesus? Maybe we should look elsewhere for a model of discipleship. Peter doesn't qualify.

Or does he?

9/21/99

Disciples of Christ

Disciples of Christ ▮

Reflect: What makes you a disciple of Christ? In what ways do you proclaim the kingdom of God? In what ways do you fail? In what ways are you like Peter?

One step time at a

Let's take a good look at what discipleship means to us. We go to church. Sometimes we pay attention to the sermon. We try to be good. At least we're kind to our friends. Sometimes we lend a hand, if our neighbors ask.

For some of us, Christian discipleship is an afterthought. After we pay the bills, we write a check for the poor. If we have time, we read our Bibles. Three weeks later, we find our children's Sunday school papers stuffed under the seat of the car. Personal devotions may be a quick prayer said on the way to work or a few minutes listening to Christian music before we find something better on the radio.

Every day, we have opportunities to talk about Jesus and to proclaim God's kingdom. What do we do? For example, suppose someone in the carpool starts talking, "You know, they ought to get them off the streets. Spreading blankets all over the sidewalk, throwing bottles in the gutter. It's a public thoroughfare. Did you ever try to walk down Church Street at noon? Every corner, there's another one begging for money. Hey, they prob'ly make more money than I do! They ought to haul them off to jail, every one of them." What do we say? How do we proclaim good news to the poor or release to the captives? Or maybe we just keep our mouths shut. After all, we don't want to make trouble. We don't want to endure the silence that follows religious pronouncements.

We're a lot like Peter aren't we? We're not holy. We don't know anything about Jesus. Even when we're offered a chance to follow, we turn tail and run. And when asked, "Aren't you a Christian?" we're apt to respond, "Yes, but—." The truth is, we are not authorities on Christian discipleship. Or are we?

Scripture

Scripture ▪

Consider: What does it mean to have a share in the new life of Jesus Christ? What does Jesus' presence in your life mean? How would you feel if you had no share with Jesus?

In the story of the footwashing, in the Gospel of John, Peter says to Jesus, "Lord, are you going to wash my feet?" Jesus answers, "Unless I wash you, you have no share with me." (See John 13:3-14.)

How would we feel if we had no share with Jesus? We rely on the presence of Jesus to get us through the hardest times. We look for eternal life, our only hope. What would we do without Jesus?

Peter says, "Lord, not my feet only but also my hands and my head." Of course he did. So would we. Though we're not always faithful, we don't want to lose the assurance of Jesus' hand in ours.

At the table of the Last Supper, Jesus says to the disciples, "The one who betrays me is with me" (Luke 22:21). The disciples looked around, wondering who will betray the Lord. "Who, me?" they ask. "Could it be me?"

Jesus answers them, "You will all become deserters." Peter is blustery: "Even though all become deserters, I will not." Jesus answers, "Before the cock crows twice, you will deny me three times." Again, Peter vows to stand his ground: "Even though I must die with you, I will not deny you." And all the disciples agreed. (See Mark 14:27-31.)

Jesus is our Lord, but we sometimes ignore his commandments. The truth is that despite our vows of loyalty, each of us knows that one way or another we have deserted and denied and betrayed Jesus. Jesus tells us, "If I, your Lord and Teacher, have washed your feet, you also ought to wash one another's feet. For I have set you an example, that you also should do as I have done to you" (John 13:14-15). How often are we willing to kneel in humility before another person? How often do we give up our ambitions to be of service? When it comes to serving one another, in Jesus' name, we're more likely to say, with Peter, "I do not know him" (Luke 22:57).

We betray Jesus for lots of reasons. We have a hard time proclaiming God's kingdom because it isn't like the world we live in. Preaching good news to the poor in a world of welfare reform and public housing seems

Take a good look at yourself. In what ways have you denied or betrayed Jesus?

Add your name to the list of people who have betrayed or denied the Lord.

like shouting in the dark. Proclaiming release to the captives is plain silly when politicians need a quota of executions to stay in office. Peter denied Jesus because he was afraid for his life. We sell out to convention; we don't want people to laugh at us.

So What?

Peter denied Jesus. All his blustery faithfulness fell flat. Asked, "Weren't you with Jesus?" he said, "I never heard of the guy." Then the cock crowed, and he broke down and cried. Maybe Peter is the disciples' disciple. He's a lot like us. He's an ordinary person badly in need of salvation.

Footwashing and Communion are symbols of salvation that point to the death and resurrection of Christ. Partaking of the bread and the cup is partaking of the death and resurrection of Christ; it is having a share in the new life that Jesus offers. Footwashing is like being "washed in the blood of the Lamb," forgiven and cleansed for all the times we deny and betray and desert the Lord.

Peter had the right idea. "Wash me, Jesus," he said. "Immerse me in your love. Give me new life." And Jesus answered, "You are clean" (John 13:10). In his death and resurrection, we are saved, clean, forgiven. And we have a share in the new life he offers.

Perhaps discipleship is simply relying on Jesus because we can't count on ourselves. Peter is a model for discipleship precisely because of his bungling enthusiasm and his lack of courage. Because he is completely inept, Peter relies on Jesus.

So What? ■

Describe Peter's relationship to Jesus.

How has learning about Peter helped to answer your questions about discipleship?

Prayer ■

Wash us, Lord. Wash away our sins. Immerse us in your love. Amen.

Session Seven

The Risen Lord

Read Matthew 28; Mark 16; Luke 24; John 20:1—21:19.

Session Focus ■

This session looks at the empty tomb as a sign that God's kingdom has come. It also considers Peter's encounter with the risen Lord. In the resurrection of Jesus we, like Peter, are forgiven, restored, called, and commissioned.

Session Objective ■

To understand discipleship in light of the Resurrection, in which we are given a share in the new life of Christ. To accept forgiveness and to begin to hear our call to proclaim the good news.

Session Preparation ■

Read the Scripture. Read through the material in this chapter. Have available copies of the order of worship used in your church.

Session Outline ■

Choose from among these activities and discussion questions.

Jesus was sentenced to death and was crucified.

After the crucifixion of Jesus, his followers were disappointed. In spite of what he had told them, they did not expect his resurrection. Early Sunday morning several women went to the tomb of Jesus to anoint the body with oils. When they arrived, they found that the stone used as the door of the tomb had been rolled away. They entered the tomb and found that the body of Jesus was not there. A young man dressed in white told them, "Do not be alarmed; you are looking for Jesus of Nazareth, who was crucified. He has been raised; he is not here. Look, there is the place they laid him. But go, tell his disciples and Peter that he is going ahead of you to Galilee; there you will see him, just as he told you" (Mark 16:6-7).

Different Accounts

In Mark, the messenger singled out Peter for emphasis. Peter had denied Jesus three times. Yet Peter repented. His tears of repentance were precious to the Lord. Jesus was concerned about Peter, so the angel mentioned Peter by name in the message. According to the tradition transmitted by Paul in 1 Corinthians 15:3-7, after the

Different Accounts ■

Read Matthew 28:1-10;
Mark 16:1-8; Luke 24:1-
12; John 20:1-10.

List the events in each account. How are they the same? different? What, do you think, would account for the differences?

Does the inclusion of particular details change the import of the account? Explain.

How do you think you might have reacted to news of an empty tomb?

Resurrection Jesus appeared to Peter. In Luke, when the women told the apostles what had happened at the tomb, they did not believe. But Peter ran to the tomb and was amazed.

In John, one of the women who discovered the empty tomb, Mary Magdalene, ran to Simon Peter and to the other disciple whom Jesus loved, probably John (John 20:2). She told them, "They have taken the Lord out of the tomb, and we do not know where they have laid him" (John 20:2). Even though the angel at the tomb told the women that Jesus had risen, Mary could not understand this. She still thought that someone had taken the body of Jesus away.

When Peter and John heard the report of the empty tomb, they ran to the tomb. John outran Peter and arrived at the tomb first. He stooped to look in and saw the linen cloths lying there, but he did not enter into the tomb. Then Peter arrived and went straight into the tomb. No reasons are given for this action of Peter. Was it because he was anxious to get close to the Lord after his denial and repentance? Was it due to his impetuous nature?

Inside the tomb, Peter saw the linen cloths lying and the napkin rolled up in a place by itself.

Then John also entered the tomb. "He saw and believed" (John 20:8). The text seems to suggest that while John believed in the resurrection of Jesus after his inspection of the tomb, Peter had not arrived at that conclusion yet.

The resurrection of Jesus was so beyond their expectation—it was such an extraordinary event—that the followers of Jesus could not comprehend it as a reality right away. All of us have somewhat similar experiences on a much smaller scale. When some unexpected, extraordinary fortune or tragic event comes our way, we cannot believe it to be true. We feel as if we were dreaming. If this is true with us, how much more it must have been true for the followers of Jesus! Resurrection from the dead was totally unexpected and miraculous.

Commissioning

Jesus appeared to the disciples many times. Peter must have been present when these appearances took place. During one of these appearances Jesus said to them, "Peace be with you. As the Father has sent me, so I send you." Then "he breathed on them, and said to them, 'Receive the Holy Spirit. If you forgive the sins of any, they are forgiven them; if you retain the sins of any, they are retained'" (John 20:21-23).

Jesus commissioned the apostles and gave them the Holy Spirit to carry on his mission.

John 21:1-23 reports an appearance of Jesus to the disciples at the Sea of Tiberias (better known as the Sea of Galilee). Jesus recommissioned Peter at that time. When Peter and six other disciples were together, Peter said to them he was going fishing. The other six joined him. They toiled all night on the Sea of Galilee but did not catch anything. Just as the day was breaking, Jesus walked along the beach; but the disciples did not recognize him. When the disciples, in response to Jesus' inquiry, told him they had not caught any fish, Jesus told them to cast the net on the right-hand side of the boat. They followed the instruction and caught a large number of fish.

At this, John recognized Jesus and told Peter, "It is the Lord!" Immediately Peter sprang into the sea and swam to the beach.

Commissioning ■

Consider: We generally think of the risen Christ as somewhat ethereal. But the Bible tells a different story. The risen Christ walked with the disciples, he built a fire and cooked breakfast and ate with them. He taught them about the Scriptures. How does reading the Gospel accounts change your perception of the risen Christ?

The beloved disciple saw Jesus on the beach and told Peter, "It is the Lord!" Reflect: How would you recognize Jesus if you met him on the street?

During many of the post-Resurrection appearances, Jesus commissioned his disciples. Discuss: In what ways do we encounter the risen Christ? What particular jobs has Jesus given us to do?

The other disciples came in the boat, dragging the net full of fish.

(According to Luke 5:1-11, when Peter first was called to discipleship, he had a similar experience. He had labored all night in vain on the Sea of Galilee. The next day, at the instruction of Jesus, Peter cast the net and caught a net full of fish.)

"Do You Love Me?" ■

Read John 21:15-19. Discuss: Was it possible, do you think, for Peter to love the Lord before the Resurrection? Why? Why not?

How do you interpret Jesus' question, "Do you love me more than these"? How does the particular interpretation of the question affect the import of the answer?

"Do You Love Me?"

When the disciples came up to the beach, Jesus had already prepared breakfast for them. After the breakfast, by the charcoal fire, Jesus asked Peter, "Simon son of John, do you love me more than these?" (John 21:15). There are three possible ways of understanding this question.

The first possibility is "Do you love me more than these men love me?" Peter had explicitly professed a devotion to Jesus that exceeded that of all other disciples. He had said, "Even though all become deserters, I will not" (Mark 14:29) and "Lord, why can I not follow you now? I will lay down my life for you" (John 13:37). Jesus may have been asking Peter whether, in light of the later events, Peter still thought he loved Jesus more than all other disciples loved him.

The second possibility is "Do you love me more than you love these friends of yours?" Peter denied Jesus, yet he stayed with those friends of his, and they went fishing together.

The third possibility is "Do you love me more than you love this fishing equipment and all that it represents?" Understood in this way, Jesus' question challenged Peter as to his entire future. Would Peter love Jesus more than he would love his own future?

Peter's behavior and actions indicated that he had not wanted a crucified Christ. But Jesus had been crucified. How would Peter's

"Do you love me? Feed my lambs" (John 21:15) sounds a lot like the Great Commandment: "Love the Lord your God—Love your neighbor" (Matthew 22:37, 39). Consider: Is it possible to love the Lord without loving neighbors?

Is it possible to love neighbors if we stand outside the love of God?

love and devotion stand in the light of the Crucifixion? Would Peter love Jesus as he was, and not as Peter wished him to be? This is an important question. Peter answered Jesus, "Yes, Lord; you know that I love you." Jesus told him, "Feed my lambs."

Jesus said to Peter a second time, "Simon son of John, do you love me?"

Peter answered, "Yes, Lord; you know that I love you."

Jesus said, "Tend my sheep." Then Jesus asked Peter the third time, "Simon son of John, do you love me?"

Peter answered, "Lord, you know everything; you know that I love you."

Jesus said, "Feed my sheep." Then Jesus predicted Peter's martyrdom and said to Peter, "Follow me." (See John 21:15-19.)

The first two times when Jesus asked Peter about his love for him, Jesus used the word *agapao* for love. The third time Jesus used *phileo* for love. In his answer all three times, Peter used *phileo* for love.

If *agapao* and *phileo* are different, the difference is not in the quality of love, but rather in the approach to or the origin of love. On this consideration, *agapao* denotes love derived from moral choice, while *phileo* connotes love derived from personal affection. Thus, the first two times Jesus asked Peter about his love of moral choice. Peter replied in each by the assertion of the personal affection that was apparently most immediately involved in his denial of Jesus. In his denial Peter turned his back directly on the person of Jesus.

In the third question, Jesus seemed to be satisfied with love of moral choice and turned to probe Peter's personal affection. Jesus wanted to draw from Peter his assurance of his love in both its forms. Peter, feeling that each form of love virtually includes the other, chose the term that would express most fully his awareness of personal love, the love his denial had violated.

Forgiven and Restored

A short time earlier, in the presence of enemies and near a fire, Peter had denied Jesus three times. Now in the presence of his friends and near a fire, he affirmed three times that he loved his Lord. This triple affirmation, accompanied by a tripled commission from the Lord, must have had the effect of giving an almost official sanction to his restoration to his place of leadership.

Believe It or Not

We all know that bodies tend to stay put. Empty tombs are the exception to every rule. If someone told us that graves were found empty or that a body had disappeared from a local funeral home, we'd suspect the messenger of having a rich fantasy life: "Yeah, right. Did the body just disappear?" We would want proof, and even seeing an empty grave wouldn't convince us. "Grave robbers, maybe."

The women went to the tomb and found it empty. An angel made the announcement: Jesus Christ is risen.

In Matthew, the chief priests spread rumors that the disciples had moved the body. In Mark, the women never told Peter and the disciples. In Luke, when the women announced that the tomb was empty, only Peter decided to find out for himself. The other disciples didn't believe, and Peter went home amazed. Amazement is something short of belief. John leaves the matter open for interpretation: When Peter found the tomb empty, did he believe? We don't know.

Forgiven and Restored ■

Many commentators suggest that Peter's threefold commission to love and tend God's sheep "undoes" or rectifies his denial. What do second chances, especially in matters of faith, mean to you?

Believe It or Not ■

Review Matthew 28:1-15; Mark 16:1-8; Luke 24:1-12; and John 20:1-18.

Pretend to be a news reporter, covering the events of Easter morning. What approach would you take? How would you begin to verify your facts? Write a short article.

Discuss: Is the empty tomb proof of the Resurrection? If you were Peter, would an empty tomb be enough to convince you of Jesus' resurrection? Is it enough to convince you? Why? Why not?

The disciples were a lot like us. They weren't sure. An empty tomb wasn't enough—not then, not now.

Second Thoughts ■

What does the empty tomb mean? What does the Resurrection mean? What does this mean to you as a disciple?

Second Thoughts

Still, the women's story raised questions. The disciples' first reaction was disbelief, and Peter was probably hoping against hope as he ran to the tomb. But what were their second thoughts? We can imagine.

What if the tomb is empty?

What would it mean if Jesus has been raised from the dead?

Maybe Jesus was right all along!

Jesus raised the dead, didn't he?

It says in the Scripture that no one will die in God's kingdom. What if Jesus is the Messiah?

What if God raised him up to rule an everlasting kingdom?

Maybe, just maybe, the Resurrection happened.

The empty tomb raised questions. The disciples must have wondered. Peter ran off to see for himself, and he went home amazed because the tomb was empty.

What About Peter? ■

Reflect: Where would you be without the Resurrection?

What About Peter?

Three of the Gospels mention Peter in connection with the story of the empty tomb. Why Peter?

Peter confessed that Jesus was the Messiah, but he couldn't accept Jesus' suffering and death (Matthew 16:13-23). He saw the Lord transformed and followed him to Jerusalem, even to the courtyard of the high priest (Mark 9:2-13; 14:66). Peter professed undying faith, but denied he ever knew the Lord. Peter's faith was at best uneasy.

Where would Peter's story end without the Resurrection? Picture the last scene:

Discuss: What does it mean to you to be forgiven? to have a share in the new life in Christ? What difference does it make in your life that Jesus is the Messiah?

Peter, huddled before an eerie fire, overcome by guilt; the first light of dawn; the voice of the crowd, "Crucify him!"; the slash of a whip; the sneering of a cynical soldier; a loud cry; the final silence of death. And Peter, alone, weeping for a dying Lord and his own lost soul.

After three days, the women went to the tomb and found it empty. Peter ran to see. Of course he did. What if the tomb were empty? What if Jesus were raised from the dead? The Resurrection gave Peter a second chance. If Jesus were raised to rule God's kingdom, Peter's sins were all forgiven and he would have a share in the new life Jesus offered.

Peter ran to the tomb and found it empty.

He Appeared to Peter, Then to the Twelve

Skim the reports of Jesus' post-Resurrection appearances (Matthew 28:16-20; Mark 16:9-20; Luke 24:13-50; John 20:19-29). What is the nature of Jesus' interaction with the believers? How do they seem to be before, then after, the appearance? What does this mean to you?

He Appeared to Peter, Then to the Twelve

The Gospel of John (21:1-22) tells about Jesus' appearance to Peter and the disciples. The disciples were fishing on the Sea of Tiberias. Jesus stood on the beach at daybreak. He told the disciples to cast their net to the right side of the boat. When Peter realized that it was the Lord, he jumped into the sea and swam to shore. The other disciples followed, hauling in a net full of fish. Jesus offered them fish and bread (John 21:13).

Then Jesus asked Peter three times, "Do you love me?" When Peter answered, "Yes," Jesus commanded, "Feed my sheep." The third time, Jesus told Peter the kind of death "by which he would glorify God. After this he said to him, "Follow me" (John 21:19).

Jesus' appearance to Peter is an act of forgiveness. Peter's encounter with the risen Lord parallels his denial. Jesus lets him know that he is part of the family of God, that he has a share in the new life of Jesus Christ.

The presence of Christ in word and sacrament lets us know that we have a share in the new life in Christ. Look at the order of worship for your church's Sunday service. Is the Lord's Supper included in the worship service? Find an act of forgiveness or pardon. At what point are you called? commissioned?

What does it mean to love the Lord?

The appearance is also Peter's call, which in the Gospel of John happens both at the beginning of Jesus' ministry and after the Resurrection. The first time, in John 1:42, Jesus says, " 'You are Simon son of John. You are to be called Cephas' (which is translated Peter)." After the Resurrection, Jesus tells Peter the kind of death he will suffer and then calls him: "Follow me." Notice: At first, Peter is named and defined by Jesus. But after the Resurrection, Peter belongs to Jesus; his death is Jesus' death. This time, Peter knows what he's getting into.

Peter's encounter with the risen Christ is also a commissioning. Jesus tells Peter, "Tend my sheep." Jesus gives Peter a job to do, to care for the people of God in Christ. The Gospel accounts of the Resurrection appearances ordinarily refer to the church: to word and sacrament (see especially Luke 24:13-53), to community (John 21:1-19), and to mission and evangelism (Matthew 28:16-20). The Resurrection is a sign of God's kingdom come. One way or another, Christian disciples are called to proclaim the good news: In Jesus Christ, God's kingdom has come.

So What? ■

Describe Peter's relationship to Jesus.

How has learning about Peter helped to answer your questions about discipleship?

Prayer ■

Jesus, come to us in word and sacrament. Forgive us. Call us. Send us out to proclaim the good news of God's kingdom; in your love, we pray. Amen.

So What?

The tomb was empty. Christ is risen. God's kingdom has come in Jesus Christ.

Like Peter, we deny and betray our Lord. Like Peter, we have a second chance. Because of the Resurrection, we are forgiven and offered a share in the new life Jesus offers.

We are also called to be disciples, to make the community of faith look like God's kingdom and to proclaim the good news. Like Peter, we rest in the assurance of Jesus' love. "Feed my sheep," says Jesus.

Session Eight

Pentecost

Read Acts 1:1-2:42.

Session Focus ■

This session focuses on the gift of the Holy Spirit as the beginning of God's new covenant; the Spirit gives life to the new creation. Discipleship means being moved—no propelled—by the Spirit to preach the good news.

Session Objective ■

To begin to experience the Spirit as the sign of God's new creation and to realize the directions in which the Spirit moves us.

Session Preparation ■

Read the Scripture. Read through the material in this chapter.

Session Outline ■

Choose from among these activities and discussion questions.

During the forty days after the Resurrection, Jesus appeared to the disciples and spoke to them about the kingdom of God. Then from Mount Olivet he ascended into heaven. Before his Ascension Jesus told the disciples to stay in Jerusalem to wait for the coming of the Holy Spirit, who would empower them to be his witnesses in Jerusalem, Judea, and Samaria and to the ends of the earth (Luke 24:45-49; Acts 1:8).

The disciples returned from the mountain of Ascension to Jerusalem. During those days of waiting the disciples probably stayed in the upper room (Acts 1:13) and met daily in the Temple (Luke 24:53). Peter seems to have acted as the leader of the group. Under his leadership they elected Matthias to take the place of Judas Iscariot in the ministry and apostleship. Since the church was to be the new Israel, symbolically at least, the number of twelve apostles, corresponding to the twelve tribes of old Israel, needed to be filled. The qualification of this one was that he should have been with Jesus throughout his entire ministry, beginning with the baptism of John until Jesus' Ascension (Acts 1:21-22).

The Gift of the Spirit

Luke writes in Acts 2:1, "When the day of Pentecost had come, they were all together

The Gift of the Spirit ■

Review the Scripture passages mentioned in this section. How would you describe the event and effects of Pentecost?

in one place." By this Luke seems to indicate that the Feast of Pentecost had prophetic significance in God's plan for redemption of the human race. Fifty days after the Feast of Passover came Pentecost. It was the feast that marked the gathering of the harvest. On that day, the disciples were gathered in. Suddenly they heard a sound from heaven "like the rush of a violent wind, and it filled the entire house where they were sitting" (Acts 2:2). And tongues as of fire appeared, distributed, and rested on each one of them. "All of them were filled with the Holy Spirit and began to speak in other languages, as the Spirit gave them ability" (Acts 2:4).

When the Holy Spirit came upon them, the disciples experienced two lasting effects. Before his Ascension Jesus told them, "You will receive power when the Holy Spirit has come upon you; and you will be my witnesses in Jerusalem, in all Judea and Samaria, and to the ends of the earth" (Acts 1:8). The first effect of being filled with the Holy Spirit was that they received power to witness for Jesus. Under the inspiration of the Holy Spirit, Peter delivered a powerful sermon that day and about three thousand people were converted.

We tend to think of the Spirit as the guiding force in our religious life. Being spiritual is what we do when we're alone and able to listen for God. Discuss: In what ways does the account of Pentecost challenge our understanding of the Spirit?

The second lasting effect of Pentecost was the cleansing of hearts. Some years later when reporting to the apostolic council what took place at Cornelius's house, Peter stated, "God, who knows the human heart, testified to them by giving them the Holy Spirit, just as he did to us; and in cleansing their hearts by faith he has made no distinction between them and us" (Acts 15:8-9). Peter testified that on the Day of Pentecost, their hearts were cleansed. James gives a good description of purity of heart in James 4:8: "Draw near to God, and he will draw near to you. Cleanse your hands, you sinners, and purify your hearts, you double-minded." Purity of heart means to be single-minded. It means to have a single goal in life—to love God with one's total person and to love one's neighbor as oneself (Matthew 22:37-39). Peter indicates in 1 Peter 1:22 that purification of soul results in love.

These two lasting effects of Pentecost are symbolized by wind and fire. In the Bible, wind usually symbolizes power and fire symbolizes purification.

After this experience of Pentecost, the disciples became courageous witnesses for Christ (Acts 2:14; 4:31; 5:29). They received power to witness so effectively that a great number of people were saved (Acts 2:41, 47; 4:4). They were endowed with power to perform mighty works (Acts 2:43; 5:12). They even rejoiced in enduring persecution for the sake of the kingdom (Acts 5:41). They lived and served in harmony (Acts 2:44).

What are ways that your community of faith witnesses to Jesus?

What is evidence of purity of heart, or single-minded devotion to God and neighbor?

Baptism of the Spirit

Luke calls this experience on the Day of Pentecost baptism with the Holy Spirit. He writes in Acts 1:4-5: "While staying with them, he ordered them not to leave Jerusalem, but to wait there for the promise of the Father. 'This,' he said, 'is what you have heard from me; for John baptized with water, but you will be baptized with the Holy Spirit not many days from now.'" Earlier John the Baptist declared, "I baptize you with water; but one who is more powerful than I is coming; I am not worthy to untie the thong of his sandals. He will baptize you with the Holy Spirit and fire" (Luke 3:16). In Acts 2:33, Peter indicates that Jesus poured out the Holy Spirit upon the disciples. Before the Day of Pentecost, Jesus had said these disciples belonged to God (John 17:6,

Baptism of the Spirit ■

The Spirit is a sign of the new creation, in which God will pour out the Spirit on all people.

How is the sacrament of baptism like the outpouring of the Spirit?

9). Jesus promised that they would be baptized with the Holy Spirit before many days. And on the Day of Pentecost, it was so.

The dispensation of the Holy Spirit did not fully commence until the Day of Pentecost. John commented, "As yet there was no Spirit, because Jesus was not yet glorified" (John 7:39). Jesus told the disciples, "If I do not go away, the Advocate will not come to you; but if I go, I will send him to you" (John 16:7). These passages indicate that the coming of the Holy Spirit in the sense of Acts 2, or the baptism with the Holy Spirit, could not take place until after the end of Jesus' earthly ministry.

After the historic Day of Pentecost, the disciples at Samaria did not receive the baptism with the Holy Spirit at the time of water baptism. Philip went to Samaria to evangelize. When the Samaritans "believed Philip [as he preached] the good news about the kingdom of God and the name of Jesus Christ, they were baptized, both men and women. . . . Now when the apostles at Jerusalem heard that Samaria had accepted the word of God, they sent Peter and John to them. The two went down and prayed for them that they might receive the Holy Spirit (for as yet the Spirit had not come upon any of them; they had only been baptized in the name of the Lord Jesus). Then Peter and John laid their hands on them, and they received the Holy Spirit" (Acts 8:12, 14-17).

During the Feast of Pentecost many pilgrims from all over the world gathered in Jerusalem. At the time of Jesus, Jerusalem normally had a population of fifty thousand. During the feasts, the population of Jerusalem would often swell to well over a million. When these people heard the sound like the rush of a mighty wind, they came

Review the Scriptures in this section. Think about it: Jesus goes away before the Spirit comes. If Jesus has gone away, how is Jesus also present in our lives?

together to the Temple court. There they heard the disciples telling in their own native languages the mighty works of God. They were bewildered at what they witnessed.

Peter's Preaching ■

Read Acts 2:14-36. What are the main points of Peter's sermon? For whom is the gift of the Spirit given?

Peter's Preaching

Under the inspiration of the Holy Spirit, Peter addressed the perplexed crowd. This address of Peter provided a model for the early Christian evangelistic sermons to the Jews. It includes four elements: an explanation of the phenomenon, a declaration of the life and ministry of Jesus, quotations from the Old Testament to substantiate the points, and a call for persons to respond to God's action.

Peter declared to them that the disciples were not drunk with wine. They were drunk with the Holy Spirit. They were under the strong influence of the Holy Spirit. This is what Peter said was prophesied by the prophet Joel. Joel 2:28 reads:

"Then *afterward*

I will pour out my spirit on all flesh" (italics added).

In citing this passage, Peter substituted "in the last days" (Acts 2:17) for "afterward." Peter as well as other New Testament writers considered the messianic age as the last days. When Jesus the Messiah came to the earth the first time, the last days had begun. In the Old Testament the Spirit of God came only upon a selected few individuals to enable them to accomplish some specific tasks. But God promised that in the future days God would pour out the Spirit upon all flesh. Then everyone who wants to could receive the Holy Spirit. This universal availability of the Holy Spirit was brought about by the death and resurrection of Jesus of Nazareth.

Peter then presented the life and ministry of Jesus of Nazareth. God did many wonder-

Write a creed or confession of faith based on Peter's sermon.

Discuss: Do you agree with Peter? Is the creed you wrote similar to other creeds of the church?

ful things through Jesus in the midst of the people hearing Peter. In the presentation of the life and ministry of Jesus, Peter put major emphasis on Jesus' crucifixion and resurrection. The crucifixion of Jesus was according to God's plan and foreknowledge. Yet those who plotted against Jesus were responsible for what they did.

However, the Crucifixion was not the final word. Jesus arose from the dead. The disciples were witnesses for the Resurrection. After the Resurrection Jesus was exalted at the right hand of God. He received from the Father the promise and poured out the Holy Spirit. Thus the pouring of the Holy Spirit that the audience saw and heard was further evidence of the Resurrection and the exaltation of Jesus. Peter said that all these events were foretold in the Old Testament, which the Jews and the Christians considered to be the Word of God.

On the basis of these evident facts, Peter called for appropriate response from the audience. They should repent and be baptized in the name of Jesus Christ so that they could receive the promise of the Holy Spirit. That day three thousand persons responded to the call and became Christians. This was the first ingathering of souls into the Christian church.

How Long, O Lord?

How Long, O Lord?

Do you ever wonder just how long it will be before God's kingdom comes?

Dream some dreams. What will the new creation be like? What will the kingdom of God be like?

After the Resurrection, Jesus appeared to many people and spoke to them about God's kingdom, God's promise of a new creation, and the baptism of the Holy Spirit. Notice: The gift of the Holy Spirit is the beginning of the new creation.

The disciples asked, "When will it happen? When will God's kingdom come?"

The truth is that we'd all like to know. We have been waiting a long time for God to keep the promise of a new creation. We have

Brainstorm. Write down all your ideas. Then, if you're feeling creative, paint or draw a mural that describes the new creation.

almost stopped dreaming of peace and good will. We cannot imagine a city where it's safe to walk, much less a city without hospitals and insurance agencies and prisons and graveyards—the necessities of our troubled age. We look for a natural world that is somehow pure, but we discover winds that take down neighborhoods and an ozone layer that is almost depleted. When will God's kingdom come? We would like to know.

But Jesus leaves the answer to God. He says only that the Spirit will come; and when it does, we will be Jesus' witnesses to the ends of the earth. His answer leaves us, like the first disciples, gaping at the heavens, wondering what on earth he meant.

Waiting ■

Discuss: What are indications that the church is waiting for the Kingdom? What is evidence that the church has lost faith and stopped waiting? Perhaps the church has confused the new creation with waiting. What do you think?

Waiting

So the apostles waited. They set up housekeeping in an upstairs room in Jerusalem, where they prayed and read the Scripture and waited. They decided that someone should be chosen to replace Judas "for he was numbered among us and was allotted his share in this ministry" (Acts 1:17). They chose Matthias, who had been with them since the baptism of Jesus and could testify to his Resurrection. Acts 1:12-26 sounds a little like the announcements on the back of a church bulletin: Choir practice Wednesday; Bible study Thursday morning; information for the newsletter should be turned in before the 25th of each month; a meeting to elect officers will be held on Sunday after church.

The disciples waited.

Pentecost ■

Tell the story of Pentecost. In a group, tell the story round robin, each person adding a sentence. Be sure to include in the story the meaning of the gift of the

Pentecost

Suddenly, with a rush of wind and fire, the Spirit of the Lord was upon them; and they began to speak, proclaiming the mighty acts of God. People heard and understood and were amazed. Jerusalem was filled with peo-

Spirit. Telling the story is a way to proclaim the good news.

ple from all over the Middle East and from as far away as Rome. Each spoke a different language. But everyone understood the little band of disciples, proclaiming God's word.

Churches today tend to be isolated. We pull away from a secular world and say our prayers behind sturdy walls and stained-glass windows. Christians sit in Sunday school rooms and tell one another about Jesus. We understand one another. But the disciples, overwhelmed by the Spirit of God, went out into the streets to proclaim the good news. They told everyone they saw about "God's deeds of power" (Acts 2:11). Of the people who heard, many believed.

**Preaching ■
the Gospel**

Discuss: In what ways do you find the new creation threatening? How do you feel about taking responsibility for Jesus' death?

Preaching the Gospel

The Holy Spirit gives people words to proclaim the good news of God's kingdom. Peter got up to preach:

Jesus of Nazareth, a man attested to you by God with deeds of power, ... this man, handed over to you according to the definite plan and foreknowledge of God, you crucified.

This Jesus God raised up, and of that all of us are witnesses. Being therefore exalted at the right hand of God, and having received from the Father the promise of the Holy Spirit, he has poured out this that you both see and hear.

(Acts 2:22-23, 32-33)

Jesus, whom *we* crucified? Wait a minute. What is Peter saying? Wasn't Jesus crucified by the Romans? Didn't the chief priests and the scribes have him arrested? We didn't do a thing. Yet Peter clearly lays the blame for Jesus' death: "Jesus of Nazareth you crucified."

Jesus was killed precisely because he proclaimed God's kingdom. Think about it. Good news for the poor means radical

Remember the good news: Jesus forgives us and gathers us into his love. God pours out his Spirit on us and gives us new life, energy, meaning, character. (Look up *spirit* in a thesaurus. You'll be amazed.)

changes in the way we live. A handout is not enough. Good news for the poor might mean leveling projects and old-wealth mansions, mixing up neighborhoods. It may mean leveling income so that everyone makes a living wage. In Luke, Jesus is clear: "Blessed are you who are poor, for yours is the kingdom of God. . . . But woe to you who are rich" (Luke 6:20, 24). Jesus came to bring peace on earth and good will among all people. He proclaimed a new social order, in which all nations stand together before God. Perhaps he meant to erase national boundaries and melt down the weapons of war. In the kingdom of God, there is no place for patriotism or military might.

Peter was right. The good news of the gospel is threatening. If Jesus came to us today, many of us would try to find a way to silence him.

But in the resurrection of Jesus Christ, we are forgiven. The risen Christ comes to us, forgives us, and pours out the Holy Spirit on us. In Christ, God makes us a new creation.

So What?
Describe Peter's relationship to Jesus.

How has learning about Peter helped to answer your questions about discipleship?

Prayer
Thank you, God, for the gift of your Holy Spirit, which gathers us into your love and makes us new. Thank you for the Holy Spirit, which pushes us into the world to proclaim the good news. Amen.

So What?

What is the Holy Spirit? The word *spirit* means life, courage, spunk, temperament, resolve, enthusiasm, self, energy, essence, meaning, power, perseverance, identity, nature, character, vigor. When the Holy Spirit is poured out on us, God gives us life, energy, meaning. Our identity is Jesus Christ. In God's kingdom, we are a new creation, defined by Jesus Christ.

The gift of the Spirit is given to us so that we will witness to Jesus Christ. Christian disciples are a lot like Peter. Overwhelmed by the Spirit of Christ, we proclaim the good news, telling everyone we meet about Jesus.

The Early Church

Read Acts 2:37–5:42.

In the early days of the church Peter provided effective leadership in many areas of church life. On the Day of Pentecost he was the main proclaimer of the gospel. Luke reports in Acts 2:42 that the believers "devoted themselves to the apostles' teaching and fellowship, to the breaking of bread and the prayers." The teaching of the apostles was the guide for Christian faith and life.

Healing in Jesus' Name

In the early days, Christians attended the Temple worship. One day Peter and John went up to the Temple at the hour of prayer, three o'clock in the afternoon. At the gate called Beautiful sat a lame man begging for alms (Acts 3:1-10).

Peter called the man to look at them and said, "I have no silver or gold, but what I have I give you; in the name of Jesus Christ of Nazareth, stand up and walk" (Acts 3:6).

Then he took him by the right hand and raised him up. Immediately the man's feet and ankles were strengthened. Leaping up, he stood and walked with the apostles into the Temple. This was his first time to enter the Temple; because of being lame he had been banned from entering the Temple. He clung to Peter and John and was walking and leaping and praising God.

originator) of new life." What does it mean to say that Peter healed in Jesus' name?

Read Acts 3:1-10, and research this story in a Bible commentary. What is the significance of such a healing? (It would, at least, require a massive reorientation of every facet of the man's life.)

All the people saw him walking and praising God and recognized him as the lame beggar who used to sit by the gate. He had been sitting by the gate for decades. Most of the people entering the Temple through that gate had seen him and had given him alms at one time or another. His face was very familiar to the people. When they saw him walking and praising God, they were astonished and amazed.

They stayed behind for a time to hear what the apostles had to say about the miracle. Peter took this opportunity to address the assembled crowd (Acts 3:11-26).

The emphasis of Peter's sermon here is that the person of Jesus is demonstrated through a miracle that, wrought in his name, revealed the power of his resurrected life. Peter first provided sufficient background about Jesus to account for the miracle. Then he explained what the mission of Jesus Christ could mean to Israel if the people would respond to him in faith.

In the sermon, Peter identifies God as "the God of Abraham, the God of Isaac, and the God of Jacob, the God of our ancestors" (Acts 3:13). This title emphasizes the covenant faithfulness of God. This faithful God promised to raise up a prophet from among the people as Moses was raised up for them (Acts 3:22-23; Deuteronomy 18:15). God promised to send a servant (Acts 3:13; Isaiah 42:1-4; 52:13—53:12). According to that promise, God did send Jesus; but Israel rejected him and had him crucified. Yet God glorified him by raising him up. "To this," Peter declares in the sermon, "we are witnesses" (Acts 3:15). Jesus is the *archegos* (author, leader, pioneer, originator) of new life.

The healing of the lame man is in the

Complete the sentence: In the name of Jesus, we. . . .

What is the role of repentance in healing?

"name" of Jesus, which is full of power. This miracle wrought in the name of Jesus is a proof that Jesus has been raised from the dead and exalted to heaven. From there he will come again to bring about all God's promises. Jesus truly is the promised Messiah. And God has sent this Messiah first to Israel.

Because of this, Israel ought to repent. If they do, Peter continues, they will receive the blessings God promised through the prophets, and they will become the source of blessings to all the families of the earth according to God's covenant with Abraham. At the end of Peter's sermon, about five thousand persons believed and became Christians (Acts 4:4).

Arrest and Warning ■

The disciples were regularly arrested, thrown in jail, and persecuted. Why were they incarcerated? What threat did they seem to present and to whom?

In our society, Christian faith is the status quo. Discuss: If we don't get into trouble for being disciples, are we actually proclaiming God's word?

Arrest and Warning

While Peter and John were still speaking to the people, the priests and the captain of the Temple guard and the Sadducees came upon them. The captain of the Temple guard was second only to the high priest in authority. Under him were officers who supervised the guards of the Temple treasuries and the gatekeepers. He was the commander of the Temple police force. His presence heralded arrest. The Sadducees were the aristocrats of Jewish political and religious powers. They jealously guarded the ancient right of the priests to teach and interpret the law and to supervise the worship in the house of God. Peter and John were not priests, but they were teaching in the Temple. They not only taught about the resurrection of the dead, which the Sadducees did not believe, but they also proclaimed the resurrection of Jesus of Nazareth, who had been crucified! So they arrested Peter and John and put them in prison overnight.

The next day the Sanhedrin, the Jewish supreme court, was called into session. The court inquired by what power and in what name they had done the miracle. Peter, filled with the Holy Spirit, declared that it was by "the name of Jesus Christ of Nazareth, whom you crucified, whom God raised from the dead" (Acts 4:10). He continued by declaring that Jesus is "the stone that was rejected by you, the builders; it has become the cornerstone" (Acts 4:11). The Jewish rulers rejected Jesus, but God made him the only way of salvation.

Many Christian churches outside the US that face regular persecution are growing; most Christian churches in the US are not. How do you explain that?

The court could not contest the fact of miraculous healing. So they threatened the apostles not to speak or teach in the name of Jesus any longer and released them. Peter declared to the court that it was more important to obey God than to obey them. First Peter 2:13-14 teaches Christians to be obedient to all human institutions. However, when the order of human authority contradicts that of God, it is more important for Christians to obey God than to obey other persons.

Ananias and Sapphira ■

Read Acts 5:1-11. Discuss: What happened to Ananias and Sapphira? Does God zap people who withhold their offerings?

Ananias and Sapphira

The Christians in Jerusalem shared not only spiritual blessings but also material goods. Those who had worldly possessions sold these from time to time and placed the money at the disposal of the apostles to be distributed among the needy in the Christian community. This was not required; but out of their love for fellow Christians, some wealthy Christians did this voluntarily. Acts 4:34-35 indicates that they did this from time to time as needs arose. One of those who did this was Joseph, named by the apostles Barnabas, which means "son of encouragement."

Do you think fear of pun-
ishment (especially for a
voluntary act) is the way
God persuades or
motivates?
Explain.

Ananias and his wife Sapphira sold a piece
of property and kept back some of the proceeds. Ananias brought only a portion of the
proceeds and laid it at the apostles' feet, pre-
tending that he brought the total amount.
Peter saw through his deception. Peter
rebuked him for lying to the Holy Spirit.
Immediately Ananias fell down and died.
About three hours later, Ananias's wife
Sapphira came in. Peter asked her whether
they sold the land for so much. She replied
that they did. Again Peter rebuked her for
conspiring with her husband to lie to the
Holy Spirit. Immediately she fell down and
died also. Because of this incident, great fear
came upon the whole church and upon all
who heard about it.

Obedience to God ■

Discuss: What are experi-
ences in which obedience
to God and obedience to
the religious or political
authorities conflict? How
do you know what God
expects?

Obedience to God

By the hands of the apostles, God did
many signs and wonders. The Christians
continued to meet in Solomon's Portico
inside the Temple court. Many people
brought sick relatives and those afflicted with
unclean spirits from all over Jerusalem and
from the towns around Jerusalem to be
healed. Peter's reputation was so great that
some even carried the sick into the streets
and laid them on beds and pallets so that as
Peter passed by his shadow might fall on
some of them.

The high priest and Sadducees were filled
with jealousy. They arrested the apostles and
put them in prison. But that night an angel
of the Lord opened the prison doors,
brought the apostles out, and told them to
stand in the Temple and speak to the people
the word of life. When the Sanhedrin met on
the following day, they sent officers to the
prison to bring the apostles out for investiga-
tion. The officers discovered the prison was

securely locked and the guards standing at the doors, but the apostles were not there.

Later they found the apostles preaching and teaching at the Temple, so they brought the apostles to the council. The high priest asked the apostles why they did not obey the earlier injunction of the council not to preach and teach in the name of Jesus. Peter spoke for the apostles, "We must obey God rather than any human authority" (Acts 5:29). Once again, Peter accused the Jewish authorities of killing Jesus, whom "God exalted... at his right hand as... Savior" (Acts 5:31).

The council members were enraged and wanted to kill them. However, Gamaliel, a Pharisee in the council, advised them to be cautious in dealing with these men. So the Sanhedrin called in the apostles, ordered them to be flogged, charged them not to speak in the name of Jesus, and let them go. The apostles left the council, rejoicing that they were counted worthy to suffer dishonor for the name of Jesus. And they continued to teach and preach Jesus as the Christ (Acts 5:12-42).

The Church, Modeled on God's Kingdom

Pentecost is the feast of the harvest. On Pentecost, the Spirit of God was poured out on the people and the word of God was preached. The Spirit and the Word gathered in the people of God, like a good harvest.

Christian disciples formed communities. They were baptized and "devoted themselves to the apostles' teaching and fellowship, to the breaking of bread and the prayers" (Acts 2:42). The early church was a lot like churches today. Congregations are defined by preaching, teaching, fellowship, sacraments, prayer, and mission.

If a Roman guard lost a prisoner, he was liable with his own life. The apostles' miraculous release could have resulted in the guard's death. Does God's call to witness ever endanger us or others? Would you take such a risk? Explain.

The Church, Modeled on God's Kingdom ■

Take a walk around your church or draw a floor plan of the church.

Read Acts 2:41-47. Identify where each of the activities listed in the Scripture takes place.

Describe the spirit of your church. (For example: Is it solemn? joyous? easy-going? self-absorbed?)

In what ways does your church reflect the kingdom of God?

Faith brings people into communities. We like to think that spirituality means being alone and quiet, listening for God's word. Doesn't faith mean retreating from the world for a little while each day and discerning God's will for our lives? The Scripture describes a different kind of spirituality: "Day by day, as they spent much time together in the temple, they broke bread at home and ate their food with glad and generous hearts, praising God and having the goodwill of all the people" (Acts 2:46-47). God speaks to us in communities. Faith, for the early church, was like a slightly rowdy family night supper, with lots of good food and laughter. Christian discipleship is a glad celebration, modeled on messianic feasts in which people come from all the ends of the earth to sit at table in God's kingdom.

The Blind See; the Lame Walk

The Blind See; the Lame Walk

In what ways does your church minister to people who are disabled? to people who are sick physically, mentally, emotionally, spiritually?

Consider each of these prayers. What does each say about faith in God's power ?

1) God, be with our brother, Sam, who is undergoing treatment for cancer.

2) God, please heal Sam as a sign of your coming Kingdom.

The Book of Acts talks about the early church as a microcosm of God's kingdom. If anyone asked, "What is the kingdom of God?" or "Who is Jesus, anyway?" Christian disciples could answer, "Come and see."

In the kingdom of God, the blind see and the lame walk. The apostles healed people. On the way to prayer in the Temple, Peter and John saw a man who was lame from birth. Peter said to him, "In the name of Jesus Christ of Nazareth, stand up and walk." Then Peter "took him by the right hand and raised him up" (Acts 3:6-7). All the people who saw were amazed.

Peter took the opportunity to preach: The man was healed in the name of Jesus, whom you crucified, whom God raised. Repent and be restored.

Why don't miracles happen today? Peter healed people; why can't we? It's a good question. The answer, I suppose, is that Peter didn't heal people. God did; and God heals where and when God chooses. Peter healed *in the name of Jesus.* Jesus was not a miracle worker, but the Messiah; he healed people as a sign of God's kingdom. So, like Peter, we pray for healing as a sign of the Kingdom; and we leave the rest to God. Why don't miracles happen today? Sometimes they do.

Good News to the Poor

The kingdom of God is good news for the poor. The believers owned everything in common. No one was needy, because people who owned property sold what they had and distributed the proceeds. Good news for the poor may mean changing economic and social structures and doing away with private property. The Book of Acts urges communal living. Good news can be pretty threatening. Imagine selling your home and property to live in a Christian community!

Freedom for the Oppressed; Release to the Captives

The first time Peter was arrested, he took the opportunity to preach. "We have acted in the name of Jesus, whom you crucified, whom God raised." The chief priests and the rulers and scribes warned Peter and ordered him to stop preaching and healing in the name of Jesus. And they released him (Acts 4:1-22).

The second time, he and the other apostles were arrested and jailed (Acts 5:17-18). But in the night, an angel of the Lord opened the prison door and brought them out to preach about Jesus. The prisoners were released: a sign of God's kingdom.

When the chief priests and the rulers tried to silence Peter, he answered them, "We

Good News to the Poor ■

In what ways does your church preach good news to the poor?

Look at your church budget. What percentage of the budget is spent on the church? What percentage is given to the poor?

How do people in the congregation offer financial support to one another?

In what ways is the church involved in changing social policy?

Freedom for the Oppressed; Release to the Captives ■

Review Acts 4:1-11. Then defend one of the following positions:

1) We've come to think of discipleship as private: just me and Jesus. By losing track of the social and political side of Christian faith, we have lost track of the true meaning of discipleship.

2) Christianity is a way of believing and living. It has to do with the uplifting and inspiration of the soul. Christian disciples should stay out of politics.

must obey God rather than any human authority" (Acts 5:29). God's authority levels all other authorities; the word of God takes precedence over law and custom.

It would be easier to live conventional lives. Proclaiming God's kingdom gets us in trouble. God's kingdom is a radically new creation; it is a new social, economic, political order. So preaching about Jesus is not sweet sentimentality. It's lobbying for change, taking on the powers that be, living by rules that are often unacceptable to society. For example, proclaiming good news may mean advocating scattered low-income housing for the poor despite the complaints of our neighbors. It may mean working against capital punishment, war, abortion, the right to carry arms—the things we do that are defined by death rather than by life. Perhaps it means befriending people everyone else avoids, even though we know that friendships label us. Proclaiming God's kingdom simply isn't acceptable.

Peter was a brave man. He took every opportunity to preach the good news.

So What?

Following Jesus means living in communities that proclaim the kingdom of God. Peter is a model of Christian discipleship. As part of the apostolic community, he proclaimed good news to the poor, he healed in Jesus' name, he lived free of human authority, he took every opportunity to preach.

Christian discipleship is not easy. How do we decide to follow Jesus? Peter said, "We cannot keep from speaking about what we have seen and heard" (Acts 4:20). If we have a share in Jesus, in the new life, perhaps we cannot help but proclaim the good news.

So What? ■

Describe Peter's relationship to Jesus.

How has learning about Peter helped to answer your questions about discipleship?

Prayer ■

God, give us your spirit so that we cannot help but proclaim the good news of Jesus Christ. Amen.

Session Ten

Gentile Missions

Read Acts 6:1–8:25; 10:1–11:30; 15:1-35; Galatians 2:11-21.

Session Focus ■
The early church dealt with issues that ultimately separated Christianity from Judaism. Among those that remain important for the church today are these: Are the Scriptures the final word, or is God still being revealed? Who should be included and excluded from the community of faith?

Session Objective ■
To address issues of discipleship that were also considered by Christians in the early church.

Session Preparation ■
Read the Scripture. Read through the material in this chapter.

Session Outline ■
Choose from among these activities and discussion questions.

The first followers of Christ were all Jews. They worshiped with the Jews in the Temple of Jerusalem. Their evangelistic outreach was confined to the Jews. Among these Jews were some Hellenists, Jews who grew up outside Palestine, spoke Greek or languages other than Hebrew, and accepted some aspects of Hellenistic culture. In time, the church launched its mission beyond Jews and Hellenists to Gentiles. This transition was brought about by the Holy Spirit and some of the leaders in the church. Peter was one of those who provided leadership.

As the number of Christians increased, the apostles could no longer take care of both physical and spiritual needs of the whole church. So seven new leaders were selected.

Moving Away From Judaism

Stephen, one of the seven, evidently evangelized in the synagogues of the Freedmen, the Cyrenians, the Alexandrians, and those from Cilicia and Asia. In the process, he disputed with the Jews who belonged to these synagogues. They accused him falsely and brought him before the Sanhedrin for trial. The accusation against Stephen was, in general, that he substituted Jesus of Nazareth for Moses and thus committed treason against

Moving Away From Judaism

Read Acts 7:2-53. Summarize Stephen's speech before the Sanhedrin.

What about Stephen's speech offended the authorities? Why, do you think, did they consider it offensive? In a similar situation, would you be willing to confess your faith?

Following Stephen's bold sermon and execution, we read that there was a great persecution. Might Stephen's sermon have been the trigger? If so, should he have been more circumspect about his witness? If our witness will cause hardship, should we reconsider offering it? Explain.

Moses and God. In particular, they said he spoke words against the Temple and the Law.

In defense, Stephen reviewed the history of God's chosen people Israel to find in it the purpose and plan of God. He traced that plan to its fulfillment in the revelation of Jesus Christ and interpreted the meaning of that revelation. So, far from treason against God, Stephen looked up to the God of glory and based his defense on God's will. He invoked the word and law of Moses, commented on the Temple, criticized the unbelieving Jews.

This is Stephen's insight: God's revelation is progressive. God's people should follow God's new revelation rather than stubbornly clinging to the former revelation. Now God's new revelation has come through Jesus of Nazareth. God's people should not stubbornly cling to the old Mosaic law and the Temple in Jerusalem. This speech of Stephen's marks the initial departure of the Christians from Judaism.

Stephen's speech outraged his audience, and they stoned him to death. A persecution of the church followed.

Philip, also one of the seven, evangelized the Samaritans. The Samaritans heard Philip's preaching, believed, and were baptized. When the apostles in Jerusalem heard about this, they sent Peter and John to Samaria. Upon arrival, they laid their hands on the believers and they received the Holy Spirit. Their mission accomplished, Peter and John went back to Jerusalem. On their way back, they preached the gospel in many Samaritan villages.

Later Peter took up an itinerant ministry, visiting churches from place to place. At Lydda he healed Aeneas who had been paralyzed and bedridden for eight years. At the invitation of Christians in Joppa, Peter went there and raised Dorcas from the dead (Acts 9:31-43).

Peter and Cornelius

Peter and Cornelius ■

Read Acts 10:1-48. What was the issue addressed in the story of Peter and Cornelius?

Cornelius was a centurion of the Italian cohort stationed in Caesarea. The Italian cohort was the auxiliary cohort raised out of Italian volunteers. So Cornelius was Italian, a Roman citizen. He was a devout man, a God-fearer. A God-fearer was one who believed in the one true God, made varying compliances with Jewish customs, yet did not accept circumcision. God-fearers were admitted to the synagogue. One afternoon during his regular prayer an angel appeared to Cornelius and told him to send for Peter.

Peter was staying in the seaside home of Simon, a tanner. Shortly before Cornelius's messengers arrived at the house, Peter went up on the housetop to pray. There he saw a vision. He saw heaven opened and something like a great sheet came down on earth. In it were all kinds of animals and reptiles and birds of the air. A voice called to him, "Get up, Peter; kill and eat" (Acts 10:13).

Use a Bible commentary or dictionary to investigate further the issue of "clean" and "unclean." Look up dietary and purity laws.

But Peter replied, "By no means, Lord; for I have never eaten anything that is profane or unclean" (Acts 10:14). The voice said to him, "What God has made clean, you must not call profane" (Acts 10:15).

This happened three times and the sheet was taken up into the sky. While Peter was pondering the meaning of the vision, Cornelius's messengers arrived and asked for Peter. The Spirit told Peter to go down to meet the three visitors.

When Peter found out the reason why these messengers came, the significance of his vision began to dawn on him. To the Jews all Gentiles were unclean. The Jews had a definite covenant with God. The Gentiles did not have this special relationship with God; they were common. The Gentiles were unclean by virtue of the Jewish law of cleanliness. For example, the Gentiles did not observe the distinction between clean and unclean meats. So no social fellowship was possible between the Jews and the Gentiles.

In the vision, God told Peter that God had cleansed these unclean Gentiles. Peter did not have to avoid association with them any longer. God wanted him to go to the Gentiles to preach the gospel.

The next day some people from Joppa accompanied Peter and they went with the messengers to Caesarea to Cornelius's house. Upon arrival Peter addressed the Gentile congregation already gathered there. He first shared his new perception of truth. "I truly understand that God shows no partiality, but in every nation anyone who fears him and does what is right is acceptable to him" (Acts 10:34-35).

Peter came to this understanding through his own vision and that of Cornelius. Surely "acceptable to God" does not mean that these persons have no need for believing in Jesus Christ. Precisely because these people were acceptable to God and needed to believe in Jesus Christ, God sent Peter to proclaim to them the message of salvation.

Peter went on to speak about the ministry, death, and resurrection of Jesus. While Peter was still speaking, the Holy Spirit fell on them all. This was another confirmation for Peter and his Jewish companions that the Gentiles had a full share in salvation. And Peter commanded these Gentile believers to be baptized.

How did Peter decide whether to baptize Cornelius and the Gentile believers? What does it mean that God shows no partiality?

What does "acceptable to God" mean? If God finds someone or something "acceptable," what obligation does that place on believers? on you personally?

What are similar issues in the church today?

Mission to the Gentiles ■

The church dealt with the question, Should members of the Christian community be held to the Mosaic covenant? How did Peter, Paul, and James respond? What was the final decision?

If you had been part of the Jerusalem council, what position would you have taken? Why?

Even when good decisions are made, we sometimes have a hard time sticking to them. Read Galatians 2:11-21. What do you think about Peter's inconsistency? Could this experience be yours? If so, how?

Mission to the Gentiles

When Peter went up to Jerusalem, the circumcision party criticized him for going to the Gentiles and eating with them. Peter told them about his vision and his experience at Cornelius's house. On the basis of these experiences, Peter argued that God had initiated the mission to the Gentiles and that he (Peter) could not withstand God.

Some of the Christians who left Jerusalem because of the persecution that arose over Stephen went to Antioch in Syria and also preached the gospel to the Gentiles there. The Lord blessed this effort and many Gentiles believed and turned to the Lord. Later Peter went to Antioch to visit and to labor for a while. While he was there he freely ate with the Gentile Christians and had good fellowship with them. However, when some Jewish Christians from Jerusalem visited Antioch, Peter withdrew from eating with the Gentiles because he feared the criticism of the circumcision party. On that occasion Paul rebuked Peter for his inconsistency (Galatians 2:11-21).

After Paul and Barnabas embarked on their first missionary journey, some of the circumcision party followed them and taught the Christians in these newly founded churches that "unless you are circumcised according to the custom of Moses, you cannot be saved" (Acts 15:1). This caused dissension in the church. So the missionaries, the apostles, and the elders met in Jerusalem to consider this issue.

After much debate at the conference, Peter stood up and claimed that the Gentiles should not be required to accept the Mosaic law. He defended this position by reciting his own experience at Cornelius's house. Barnabas and Paul related what signs and wonders God had done through them among the Gentiles. Finally James, the brother of the Lord, concluded that Gentile Christians should not be required to accept the Mosaic law (Acts 15:13-21). However, they should be requested to abstain from the pollutions of idols, from unchastity, from eating what is strangled, and from eating blood. These four things were most repulsive to the Jews.

This decision seemed good to the Holy Spirit and the leaders of the church. So the leaders communicated this decision to the Gentile Christians in Antioch, Syria, and Cilicia. Finally the church came to realize that the Gentiles did not have to accept Judaism in order to become Christians.

Growing Pains

Growing Pains ■

How is your church similar to the early church? How is it different?

How were decisions made in the early church? How are they made in your church?

We tend to think that the early church was unified. The Christians faced a secular world that was at best ambiguous about the church; persecutions were a normal occurrence. But at least disciples of Christ were united in faith. Unfortunately, our picture of the early church doesn't jibe with the Scriptures.

Peter and the apostles started the church by preaching the gospel. As more and more people were gathered into communities of faith, leaders made decisions that would change the church's doctrine and its composition.

New Revelation

New Revelation ■

Defend a position:

1) The Bible is God's Word and is authoritative for faith and life. Nothing should be added to or taken away from the revelation of Scripture.

Stephen was a newly appointed leader in the church and an evangelist. As he preached the gospel, Jewish religious leaders collected evidence. Finally, he was brought before the Sanhedrin, tried, convicted, and executed.

Stephen was accused of saying that "Jesus of Nazareth will destroy this [holy] place and will change the customs that Moses handed

2) The Bible is God's word, but God is revealed in many ways, both within the community of faith and in contemporary culture. The Bible is helpful and necessary for evaluating new revelation.

on to us" (Acts 6:14). He was accused of replacing Judaism with Christianity.

Stephen responded by confessing his faith. He told about God's revelation to the people of Israel, beginning with Abraham, Joseph, Moses, David. The covenant between God and God's people was established long before the Temple, the holy place, was built. Stephen accused the religious leaders of hypocrisy. Though they revered the Law, they did not obey it. They persecuted prophets who spoke God's word and foretold the coming of the Messiah. Stephen told the story of faith beginning with Abraham and ending with a vision of Jesus Christ seated at the right hand of God. He asked the religious leaders to believe not only "the customs that Moses handed on" but God's new revelation in Jesus Christ (Acts 6:14).

And "they became enraged and . . . dragged him out of the city and began to stone him" (Acts 7:54, 58).

Stephen's confession doesn't sound especially threatening. It sounds like the creeds of the church: "I believe in God . . . and in Jesus Christ." But Stephen asked religious people to accept new revelation.

Read Acts 7:51-53. Why did Stephen tell the Sanhedrin that they and their ancestors opposed the Holy Spirit?

We can understand why Stephen was stoned. Consider: We believe that our Scriptures are sacred and are the source of what is necessary and sufficient for salvation. The Holy Spirit provides the guide for our faith and practice. What would happen if someone told us that our Bible, though true, is insufficient? How would we feel if we were told that Christians throughout history have been hypocritical and unyielding? If someone told us that God has revealed something new, so close to God's heart that rejecting the new belief is certain damnation, and that we have rejected it, what would we say? The truth is we don't like change. We believe the Scriptures, and we believe tradition; but we have a hard time with the idea that God works in communities in today's world. We don't like our customs challenged.

Stephen challenged the customs of the Jewish community. At the same time, he asked the religious leaders to look at God's new revelation in Jesus Christ. In Stephen's speech are the first inklings of change in the Christian church, as the Christian community began to pull away from Judaism.

Church Politics

Church Politics ■

Make a list of people who should be included in the church. Then make a list of who should be excluded. Explain why you would include some people and exclude others.

Read Acts 10:15, 34-42; 11:17; 15:6-11. After reading the Scripture, would you change your lists? Why? Why not?

The church was in turmoil. Should the Christian community include Gentiles as well as Jews? If so, should Christians abide by the Mosaic law? The questions were not easy to answer. They involved making decisions about who was in and who was out of the church and about the faith and practice of the Christian community.

Some people said that Gentiles, if they were to be included, must abide by all Judaic laws. Some said that Gentiles could be included with or without obedience to the Law; and furthermore, the Law should be relaxed for the Christian community as a whole. Others took a position somewhere between the two extremes.

Peter, who was a good Jew, had a vision; and he heard a voice, saying, "What God has made clean, you must not call profane" (Acts 10:15; 11:9). He understood the vision to mean that God approved the church's mission to the Gentiles. Later, he was convinced that the Gentiles need not be bound by the law. "On the contrary," he said, "we believe that we will be saved through the grace of the Lord Jesus, just as they will" (Acts 15:11).

The conflict that began in the early

Though we consider the Bible to be God's Word, we are apt to understand parts of the Bible to be authoritative. Others we find reason to ignore. For example, we accept the Ten Commandments as God's law, but we do not obey all the food laws.

Discuss: What are our standards for making judgments about the Scripture? How do we decide if a particular passage of Scripture is authoritative for our lives?

So What? ■

Describe Peter's relationship to Jesus.

How has learning about Peter helped to answer your questions about discipleship?

Describe your relationship with Jesus. How has it changed?

Prayer ■

God, prepare us for new life in your kingdom. Make us disciples. Give us words to proclaim the good news of Jesus Christ our Lord and our Savior. Amen.

church is not resolved. Christians still struggle with who should be welcome and who should be excluded from the community of faith. We still consider the law authoritative, though we pick and choose the laws we obey.

Churches include and exclude people simply because of custom, tradition, location, denomination, social status, race, age, dress. Churches also struggle with issues of morality and with whether to include people they consider immoral or profane. The Bible is used to justify both including and excluding groups of people.

So we actually have two problems: (1) Who's in and who's out? How do we decide? and (2) What parts of the Bible do we accept as authoritative?

Early Christians decided to include the Gentiles, but they compromised on the extent to which Christians should be bound by the Law. When we look to Scripture for answers, perhaps we should pay attention to Peter: "We believe that we will be saved through the grace of the Lord Jesus, just as they will" (Acts 15:11).

So What?

We started out asking questions: What is discipleship? What should we believe? How should we act? If we take seriously the idea that Peter and the first Christians are models of Christian discipleship, then we need to take a long look at ourselves and to answer new questions. Are we open to God's new revelation? Are we willing to welcome into the church all of God's people? Are we willing to proclaim the good news of God's kingdom in all that we say and do? Are we willing to have a share in the new life Jesus offers?